The Christian Prenuptial Agreement

The Power of Marriage Unleashed

Copyright © 2014 Patricia Hartman. All Rights Reserved.

Patricia Hartman
1729 NW 36 Court, Oakland Park, FL 33309
(954) 731-9538
www.ChristianPrenuptial.com

The Christian Prenuptial Agreement:
The Power of Marriage Unleashed

By Patricia Hartman, Author

Printed in the United States of America

ISBN 978-0-9825818-5-8

The author guarantees that, except as otherwise noted, all content is original and does not infringe upon the legal rights of any other person or work. No part of this book may be reproduced in any form without permission of Patricia Hartman. The views expressed in this book are not necessarily those of the publisher.

All scripture quotations, unless otherwise indicated, are taken from the Holy Bible, New International Version®, NIV®. Copyright ©1973, 1978, 1984, 2011 by Biblica, Inc.™ Used by permission of Zondervan. All rights reserved worldwide. www.zondervan.com. The "NIV" and "New International Version" are trademarks registered in the United State Patent and Trademark Office by Bilica, Inc. ™

Published by Blackstone Media Group, www.BMGcreative.com

To My Bridegrooms

I dedicate this book to The Bridegroom, Jesus Messiah. On bended knee, He proposed to me, offering me eternal life with Him. He agreed to pay off all the debts I had carelessly accumulated—and continue to incur in pursuit of my own selfish desires—so that I could live an abundant life together with Him forever. He loved me when I didn't deserve to be loved. He surrendered all, including His life, so that I could live victoriously. In saying "yes," I entered the ultimate prenuptial agreement. May I always honor Him in taking His name, "Christian."

I further dedicate this book to my husband, Patrick, who on bended knee, proposed to me, promising to love me and be responsible for me and our family. He has demonstrated godliness and sacrifice each day of our walk together. He loves me when I don't deserve to be loved. His life is a demonstration of sacrificial love. He has actively participated in the production of this book by listening and loving me through the process. He co-labors with me in marriage ministry. Thank you for loving me with such tenderness and care. Thank you for encouraging me. I love you. In saying "yes," I entered the second greatest prenuptial agreement of my life. May I always honor God and you through our marriage and in taking your name, "Mrs. J. Patrick Hartman."

4

Contents

Chapter 1 – Introduction -- *Unleashing the Power*   **11**

Part I – Discovery   **19**
Chapter 2 – A Prenuptial Mandate?   21
Chapter 3 – History and Overview of Prenups   27
Chapter 4 – The Power of the Prenup   35
Chapter 5 – Impact of Secular Law   59
Chapter 6 – What Does God Want for You?   79

Part II – Practical Application   **105**
Chapter 7 – How To Put It All Together   109
Chapter 8 – What To Include   115
Chapter 9 – How To Get It Done   141
Chapter 10 – Final Thoughts   149

Part III – Preparation Exercises   **155**
1. Writing Your Marriage Vows   158
2. What Will Your Lives Count For?   160
3. Rules of Engagement   162
4. Writing Your Statement of Faith   166
5. Financial Planning   170
6. Keeping In-Laws from Becoming Out-Laws   174
7. Do You Really Mean "For Better or Worse"?   182
8. A Tale of Two Households   188
9. What Are You Going To Do about This?   196

Appendix 221

Here Comes The Bridegroom	223
The Chemistry of Love	227
As It is Written, so Shall It Be Done	235
What Is Divorce and Family Fragmentation	
CostingYou?	249
Sample Christian Prenuptial Agreement	253

References and Acknowledgments 271

Sources	271
Acknowledgements	277
Author Bio	279
Endnotes	281

Preface

"You *are* going to have a prenup, aren't you?"

That was the question my divorce-attorney friends asked me when I got engaged in 2006. It was more an insistence than a question. Some even offered to prepare it for free. Why would they do that?

I work with them as a forensic[1] CPA in the divorce arena. Every day we witness couples going to battle over their property and children. Every day we see outcomes that may not seem fair. My friends just wanted to protect me. After all, they knew how hard I had worked to get where I was. They didn't want to see me lose everything I had worked for "if things didn't work out." They knew the depth of my losses when my ex-husband had left me years earlier. They believed that both my fiancé and I had kids who needed their inheritances protected. From their viewpoint, no one should marry without a prenup.

Should I have had a prenup?

I believed it was my Christian duty to decline. I thanked my friends for their gracious offers, explaining that the premise of a prenup contradicted my faith. For example, Christians marry for life, so having a prenup would be like divorce planning. Prenups show a lack of trust in the person you are marrying. They also indicate a lack of trust in God to provide for you in the event of divorce. No prenup for me. End of story.

I was wrong. It's not that I shouldn't have had a prenup; it's that I shouldn't have had a *secular* prenup. Secular prenups contradict the vows that I took and what God intended for

7

marriage. It was right not to have a secular prenup but wrong not to have a Christian prenup.

The problem was there didn't seem to be such a device. When I asked pastors about prenups, they just said "no." But their ideas about prenups were related to secular documents that Christians attempt to use — documents that lack fundamental Christian beliefs and precepts.

As I searched the web, I didn't find any Christian prenups. Most of the internet research revealed articles that just said "no" to Christians using prenups.

The Christian prenup's time has come. It provides a spectrum of benefits to both the couple and to our society. It brings marital stability to this new generation. It counters the attack on Christian values and the increasing hostility by our secular society against those values. Divorce laws make it easy to bail on marriage and rarely uphold Christian vows. Using a Christian prenup, we can undo much of the damage that the laws impose.

Unfortunately, professing Christians get divorced at the same rate as non-believers. There should be a difference. We need to approach marriage in a fresh new way, and it starts with you. This generation can turn the tide to return marriage to the societal foundation that God intended.

Your Christian prenup may be the very document that holds your marriage together when life gets tough. It's a declaration of all that you profess to believe and hope to accomplish. When fully integrated with God's design and principles, it unleashes a power to not only get you through the tough times, but also to enable you to enjoy every minute of the journey.

Ultimately, it will be a document that honors God and your spouse, helping to guide your marriage so it produces results that will count for eternity. And isn't that what we all want — a life that is not wasted? May it be said of you when you leave this earth, "They were an amazing couple. They left a godly legacy and touched hundreds of people's lives."

Legal Disclaimers

I am not an attorney. I am not offering legal advice.

Therefore, nothing contained anywhere in this book should be construed as legal advice. Consult with an attorney for all points of law prior to entering into any prenuptial agreement to ensure its enforceability under the law.[2]

This book contains discussions on various aspects of law that have been researched and garnered from information readily available to the public. I am a forensic CPA[3] who routinely works in matrimonial law. My remarks regarding the law are my own opinions and observations. These discussions and remarks should *not* be construed as legal opinions. How you proceed with the preparation of your prenup is your choice and should be done advisedly, with much prayer and supplication.

Laws of individual states control the formation and dissolution of marriages. Those laws are in a constant state of flux. The laws of your state may be significantly different than those presented in this book. Your state laws must be carefully considered before entering into marriage. I urge you to consult with an attorney regarding your state's laws and the implications of secular law on your marriage.

You may be tempted to prepare your prenup without a lawyer and/or by using a do-it-yourself website, especially if you are not concerned with its enforceability under the law. Beware that any document you create may become evidence later. The provisions of your prenup may have unintended consequences that could cause you serious legal problems.

LEGAL DISCLAIMER

Utilizing this book or any of its recommendations is no guarantee for marital success or for legal enforceability of any prenuptial agreements that you prepare and execute. The information in this book is provided to give you basic information for your discussions related to the terms of your prenuptial agreement. Examples of various circumstances are provided for illustrative purposes. They are oversimplifications of complex issues. There is nothing simple about the law, and there may be exceptions and extenuating circumstances that must be considered when preparing a legal document.

The author takes no responsibility for any outcomes either in your marriage or in the enforceability of your prenuptial agreement that result from using this book and/or its information. It is your responsibility to pray, seek God, seek godly counsel, compare the information to the Word of God, and seek the assistance of an attorney to handle legal matters.

1

Introduction

Unleashing the Power

How do you have a great marriage? That depends upon how you define a great marriage. Have you and your fiancé determined what you expect from marriage and what would make it great? If used correctly, a prenup can be a powerful tool for helping you accomplish what you set out to do when you got engaged — have a great marriage.

Pursuit of a great marriage is a higher purpose than what is often intended for prenups. They are usually no more than the Plan B for when things don't go well. You might even say they are plans for failure. No one wants their marriage to fail. As a result, it's time for a new and radically different approach to marriage that will unleash the power that God intended for your marriage — Plan A.

A radical idea requires a paradigm shift for those who will be affected by it: engaged couples, attorneys, and pastors. I include pastors because pastors have historically rejected modern secular prenups. And rightly so. Modern secular prenups focus on how to protect parties' self-interests and rights. This attitude is consistent with the secular mantra, "It's all about me." However, a truly Christian prenup focuses on honoring God with our marriage, becoming one flesh, sacrificially loving each other — especially when we are unlovable — and forgiveness, forgiveness,

THE CHRISTIAN PRENUPTIAL AGREEMENT

forgiveness. This is a paradigm shift from self-protection to self-sacrifice. When we honor God, the blessings flow.

In addressing this radical approach to prenups, different readers will have specific informational needs. Couples who have never been married will have different concerns than those who may have been married before. Pastors will be seeking a scriptural basis for their paradigm shift. Attorneys may need information related to what a Christian prenup should contain that makes it different from a secular agreement.

This information is packed into Part I, with some topics expanded by reference in the Appendix. While preparation exercises are called for throughout the book, they are conveniently located in one section (Part III) for easy use. As such, the book is laid out as follows.

Part I	Discovery (What You, Your Pastor, and Attorney Need to Know)
Part II	Practical Application (How to Get It Done)
Part III	Preparation Exercises (Building Material)
Appendix	Sample Prenup and Expanded Topics

Already Married?

Postnuptial agreements are just like prenups except that they are used by those who are already married. You can derive the same wonderful, God-honoring purposes by preparing a postnup.

Literary License

Throughout the book, I use the masculine version of the word *fiancé* to describe both men and women because it is distracting to the reading flow to include a denotation such as "fiancé(e)."

12

INTRODUCTION: UNLEASHING THE POWER

Maximize Your Benefits

Writing your prenup is a process. It starts with gathering information provided in this book. It also includes discovering what you and your fiancé want for your marriage and for your lives together, such as career expectations, child rearing, and retirement. Ultimately, you will incorporate that information into your agreement so that it is a comprehensive — as well as God-honoring — document on which you can build a rock-solid marriage.

To maximize your benefits, I suggest using this book as follows:

1. Determine: What's a homerun?

Before endeavoring on any worthwhile venture, it is critical to define together what you expect and want for your marriage. What are your mutual goals? Is there a couple who comes to mind when you think of an ultimately successful marriage? You might even want to interview them to find out what it takes to have a successful marriage. What would be a "homerun" for both of you? Take time now to discuss this with your fiancé and then make some notes about the factors and goals that you believe need to be present to create a homerun.

The plans of the diligent lead to profit as surely as haste leads to poverty (Proverbs 21:5).

2. Don't take shortcuts.

Take the time to work through the process. It will help you to develop new muscles needed for building a godly marriage and hitting that homerun. As with any workout at the gym:

13

THE CHRISTIAN PRENUPTIAL AGREEMENT

*No discipline seems pleasant at the time, but painful.
Later on, however, it produces a harvest of righteousness and
peace for those who have been trained by it (Hebrews 12:11).*

Some of the information may take time to digest. Not only is
the process important to writing your prenup, but you will also be
practicing life-long skills that will ensure open and effective
communication. Open and effective communication is essential to
trust and happiness.

3. Seek to learn all you can about each other through the process.

There are a number of Preparation Exercises provided in Part
III. These will be referenced throughout the materials. As you
work through them, you will discover much you did not know
about each other. Use those exercises to amend the vision you cast
for your homerun.

After interviewing hundreds of couples, it's safe to say that
virtually all of us are "unconscious incompetents" when we first
get married. I know I was. That title is not meant to be insulting. It
simply means that you don't know what you don't know.[4] It can be
as matter of fact as not knowing your spouse's medical history
when you have to rush them to the emergency room in the middle
of the night a few months after your wedding. (This happened to
me). It's not that you don't care; it's that you just didn't realize you
didn't know, and therefore would not have thought to ask.

Imagine wanting to add a second story to a house that you just
bought — a house that's more than twenty-five years old. Can the
foundation handle the extra weight? How's the wiring and
plumbing? Are there lurking dangers caused by make-shift
improvements done by the previous owners? You will want to
have inspections to find faulty workmanship so you can correct it
before you build. Only then can you plan and build a solid home
that will last for years.

INTRODUCTION: UNLEASHING THE POWER

"They are like a man building a house, who dug down deep and laid the foundation on rock. When a flood came, the torrent struck that house but could not shake it, because it was well built. But the one who hears my words and does not put them into practice is like a man who built a house on the ground without a foundation. The moment the torrent struck that house, it collapsed and its destruction was complete" (Luke 6:48-49).

What *don't* you know about marriage and your fiancé? What do you think you know that may be wrong? Almost all conflict in marriage stems from a lack of information, wrong information, faulty assumptions, and unrealistic expectations. Unchecked, these gaps in information and communication can send your marriage to the brink of divorce.

4. Don't try to get it all done in one sitting.

Break it down and deal with the topics raised in a series of sessions. Reflect on what you read. Discuss each section with your fiancé, sharing what you learned or if something changed your thinking or your ideas about your marital homerun.

5. As you read, keep a list of things that are important for you.

After you have completed the first six chapters, you should have a pretty good list of what you would like included in your prenup. This will make it easier when you get to Part II where you put it all together.

15

THE CHRISTIAN PRENUPTIAL AGREEMENT

Blessing

May God be with you and grant you wisdom as you seek to honor His plan and purpose for your marriage so that you will hit a marital homerun.

Part I

Discovery

What You, Your Pastor, and Attorney Need to Know

*The heart of the discerning acquires knowledge,
for the ears of the wise seek it out
(Proverbs 18:15).*

Overview of Part I - Discovery

Chapter 2   A Prenuptial Mandate?

Chapter 3   History and Overview of Prenups

Chapter 4   The Power of The Prenup

Chapter 5   Impact of Secular Law

Chapter 6   What Does God Want for You?

A Prenuptial Mandate?

Calling a Christian prenuptial agreement a mandate might seem bold, but when you consider what God has revealed in Scripture, the call becomes clear. Scripture says:

- We must honor our covenants and vows.

- We are not to be conformed to this world.

- We are to follow God's laws and precepts for marriage.

- God had His covenants recorded in His Word.

The Legally Mandated Writing

Legally, the only written document generally required for marriage is the marriage license. Prior to the wedding, the bride and groom apply for and receive their license according to their state's laws. After the wedding ceremony, the officiator, the couple, and witnesses sign it. It's almost as if the couple enters a

THE CHRISTIAN PRENUPTIAL AGREEMENT

marriage contract with the state because, by default, they are agreeing to state laws — even if those laws contradict God's laws and premises. Glenn Curran, a Christian attorney friend and biblical scholar, said it this way:

> When a Christian lives in a land that has laws that are, or may become, contrary to Scripture, and when that Christian is allowed to avoid those laws in favor of scriptural laws and precepts by merely writing them down and signing them, does that Christian not have a duty to do so?[5]

Is Talk Cheap?

Except for signing the marriage license, the agreements made at a Christian wedding are generally all spoken. But do we really understand the implications of what we are promising or are we just going through the motions? Consider the agreements made during the typical ceremony:

- A grown-up little girl fulfills her childhood dreams for the most romantic and important day of her life.
- Parents go broke making it happen.
- With a tear in his eye, a father lets go of his little girl by giving her to the groom.
- The couple exchanges vows, which usually go something like this:

> I, _____, take you, _____, to be my lawfully wedded wife/husband, to live together in the Holy Estate of Matrimony: to love, honor, respect, trust, cherish, encourage, and support you according to God's Holy ordinance, forsaking all others and keeping myself only unto you, for better or worse, for richer or poorer, in sickness and in health, in good times and in bad, in joy and in sorrow, in failure and in triumph, from this day forward until death do us part.

A PRENUPTIAL MANDATE

- The wedding guests agree to support and pray for the couple.
- The couple exchanges rings, saying: "With this ring, I thee wed. And with all my worldly goods, I thee endow."
- The pastor fulfills his obligation to state laws by solemnizing the ceremony and pronouncing them husband and wife. The pastor then says, "What God has joined together, let no man put asunder."
- The pastor authorizes the new husband to kiss his bride, which he does gladly.
- The pastor presents the new couple as "Mr. & Mrs. _____."

During your ceremony, you accept an assignment: making promises to love your spouse until death, pretty much no matter what. You agree to enter the Holy Estate of Matrimony according to God's Holy ordinance. This means you will be guided by God's laws and precepts. You agree to give all you own to your spouse. Are you sure you understand the implications of what you are promising? Saying it is one thing, but are you willing to put that in writing? Shouldn't you be?

Why do you suppose God thought it important to record His covenants with us? He could have left His covenants, promises, and story to the oral traditions. Instead God pressed Moses into service as His first official scribe. He had Moses write the first five books of the Bible (the Pentateuch), which include man's history from the beginning, several of God's covenant promises, His faithfulness to those promises, and His law.

God indicates the importance of what He has recorded in a number of places. For example:

*Jesus answered, "**It is written**: 'Man shall not live on bread alone, but on every word that comes from the mouth of God' " (Matthew 4:4, emphasis added).*

23

THE CHRISTIAN PRENUPTIAL AGREEMENT

> *When the Lord finished speaking to Moses on Mount Sinai, He gave him the two tablets of the covenant law, the tablets of stone **inscribed by the finger of God** (Exodus 31:18, emphasis added).*

God teaches us that marriage is a picture of our relationship with Him. Jesus is the Bridegroom and we, the Church, are His Bride.[6] He has proposed to us, offering us eternal life with Him should we choose to accept. He is preparing a mansion for us in Heaven. In the fullness of time, He will be returning for us, His Bride, to take us to the marriage banquet. He has recorded His prenuptial agreement with us in His Word, so that we can know that we know the truth.

The Appendix contains a piece called "So It Is Written, so It Shall Be Done." It explores a host of other reasons why writing a prenup solidifies and forms a firm foundation for a marriage. But the bottom line is this: putting our covenants and commitments in writing helps to clarify our promises and assures our spouse of the heartfelt commitment we have to God and to them.

Have you decided what vows you plan to take?

 Take some time to do the Preparation Exercise 1: "Writing Your Marriage Vows."

Taking Up the Mantle

Based upon God's revelations in Scripture, Christians have a duty to write a prenuptial agreement to acknowledge their vows and covenants that follow God's laws and precepts, rejecting the counter-Christian laws and culture as a witness to the glory of God. We have a duty to right the wrongs that exist or may be imposed by the government. Further, God recorded His covenants as a

A PRENUPTIAL MANDATE

witness to His commitment and love for us in His Word. In the same way, we have a duty to record our covenant agreements as a witness to our commitment and our love for one another.

Are you ready to take up the mantle and put your promises in writing?

Blessing

May God give you the strength and courage to take up the mantle and honor God by committing to honor your spouse.

THE CHRISTIAN PRENUPTIAL AGREEMENT

History and Overview of Prenups

* * * * *

A couple had been married for 50 years and had raised a brood of ten children and was blessed with 20 grandchildren. When asked the secret for staying together all that time, the wife replied, "Many years ago we made a promise to each other: the first one to pack up and leave has to take all the kids."

* * * * *

Prenuptial agreements are written documents between two adults that set out the terms of their marriage and/or divorce. Sometimes people who are already married decide to enter similar agreements after the wedding. These are called postnuptial agreements. Most couples use modern secular prenups as protection devices in the event of divorce. Some couples also use them to set a general course for marriage. Commonly, prenups contain provisions for:

THE CHRISTIAN PRENUPTIAL AGREEMENT

- Ownership and management of assets, including family businesses

- Pre-marital debt protection and post-marital debt management

- Children from prior relationships

- Filing of tax returns

- Spouse's college education

- A surviving spouse

- Financial support and property division in the event of divorce

Because states are primarily interested in the welfare of children as a result of divorce, they usually do not allow prenups to limit certain children's issues such as visitation or basic child support.

Some couples include issues that may not be enforceable by a court, such as how often they will have sex or who will do certain household duties. Some issues, while perhaps not enforceable, may help a judge understand the couple's intentions when they got married and perhaps craft a ruling that will uphold those intentions to the greatest degree possible under the law. An attorney can help direct you in these matters.

1. History of Marriage Contracts

Marrying with a prenup is not a modern phenomenon. Originally, prenups were used to convey women and property. In fact, women were considered a form of property. Parents were

HISTORY AND OVERVIEW OF PRENUPS

responsible for their daughters until they were married. Vestiges of this are still evident in wedding ceremonies when the pastor asks, "Who gives this woman to be married to this man?"

Historically, marriages have been arranged by parents. (They still are in some cultures.) The parents often drew up marriage contracts that they signed when the couple was betrothed or at the wedding ceremony.

Some parents employed professional matchmakers to maximize the benefits of particular marriages. In Genesis 24, Abraham sent his servant to find a wife for his son, Isaac. Abraham wanted to honor God by ensuring that Isaac would not marry a Canaanite, but rather a daughter from his father's clan. Guided by God, the servant found Rebekah. The servant then negotiated the financial arrangements for her and brought her back to Isaac.

In some respects, the system of parents picking prospective mates works better than picking your own mate. Parents often make better choices for their children than children do for themselves because parents want what is best for their children. Parents usually choose someone of the same background, upbringing, and ethnicity. They look for financial stability and responsibility. In contrast, children's decisions are too often based only on romantic feelings, without regard to the realities of what it takes to have a lasting marriage.

The way of fools seems right to them, but the wise listen to advice (Proverbs 12:15).

Ironically, marriage contracts and prenuptial agreements often gave property rights to the wife. It's ironic because prenups today often keep women from having a claim on their husband's property. Since women had no property rights themselves, they were reliant on husbands and parents for housing and meeting economic needs. A divorce from or death of a husband could equate to a death sentence for the wife.

THE CHRISTIAN PRENUPTIAL AGREEMENT

This type of prenuptial agreement is still used in the Orthodox Jewish faith. Before the wedding ceremony couples sign a "ketubah." While non-Orthodox Jewish families may use contemporary documents that are often flowery expressions of love, traditional ketubahs are marriage contracts ...

> ... by which a bridegroom obligates himself to provide a settlement for his wife if he divorces her, or his heir if he predeceases her ... From the root katav, "to write," [it] is the name for both the written contract itself and for the amount the husband is obliged to settle on his wife. The main purpose of the ketubah is to prevent a husband [from] divorcing his wife against her will, which, in talmudic times, he had the right to do. The knowledge that he had to pay his wife her ketubah would serve as a check against hasty divorce.[7]

Along with the prenup, there were often payments made to or from the parents for the daughter. "Consideration" is a term used in contract law that means something of value given in return for another item of value. Items of value can mean promises to perform. Because women were property, it is not surprising that there were payments made between or by the parents, depending upon the traditions and laws of the area. In our example of Isaac and Rebekah in Genesis 24, the servant gave precious gifts to Rebekah and her family when they agreed to her marriage. Marriage payments took three forms:

Bride price: Money or property paid by the groom or his family to the parents of the bride.

Dowry: Money paid to the groom or used by the bride to help her establish a household. A trousseau is a form of dowry. It usually consists of linens and clothing saved for marriage by the bride.

Dower: Property given to the bride by the groom at the time of the marriage that was to be used by the bride to support herself in case she outlived her husband.

30

HISTORY AND OVERVIEW OF PRENUPS

Engagement rings, depending upon your state, may be viewed as either a gift or consideration on a contract. In the case of a gift, it may be viewed as conditional or unconditional, the difference being whether it must be returned in the event the groom does not marry the bride. If it is determined to be unconditional or a gift, then the bride may be able to keep it regardless of the outcome.

(For a more detailed explanation of the historical betrothal process, see the Appendix: "Here Comes The Bridegroom.")

2. Secular v. Christian Prenups

Modern American prenups commonly protect a person with assets from someone who doesn't have assets. They are usually self-centered, focusing on how to protect the party with more to lose. Even though couples may promise to love one another until death parts them, with virtually no conditions, there are usually unspoken conditions that underlie those promises, like: *so long as you keep a clean house,* or *so long as you are attentive to me.* It is unlikely that even the couple realizes their commitment's lack of depth. The underlying promise of most prenups is:

Secular Prenup:

> I promise to stay married as long I feel loved. If things don't work out, then we each take what we came with and return to where we came from.

While not stated outright, the unspoken words eliminate — or at least minimize — the consequences of abandoning the marriage. You need to ask yourself: *Is this the commitment that you expect when you marry?* Don't you want someone who is 100% vested in making your marriage work? The couple entering this type of agreement is not "all in." In fact, you might say this is essentially another form of living together.

31

THE CHRISTIAN PRENUPTIAL AGREEMENT

In the preface, I explained that my divorce-attorney friends asked if I was going to have a prenup. At first I just said, "No." But then I had a thought: *What about a Christian prenup?* What if there was a prenup that captured what we were really promising at the altar? The next time an attorney asked me about using a prenup, I answered, "Yes, and mine would say..."

Original Christian Prenup Idea:

> I promise to love, honor, and cherish for life. However, if you leave me or cheat on me, I get everything.

They all laughed and said, "Nobody would sign that." But, in truth, isn't that exactly what Christian couples are promising when they say their vows? As Christians we commit to love, honor, and cherish, for better or worse, for richer or poorer, in sickness and in health, in good times and bad, in triumph and in failure, until death do us part. And then we say: "With this ring I thee wed, and with all my worldly goods, I thee endow." That is a far cry from the secular prenup that says, "I get to keep my stuff."

While my original thought captured the seriousness of the commitment, there was one important missing element: personal responsibility. I can only be responsible for one person: me. When Christians marry, they are agreeing to love regardless of how their spouse acts. Further, they are agreeing to love as Christ loved the Church. He died for us because we are sinners, not because we behave well or are lovable. Recognizing that I can only be responsible for my own actions caused me to change the perspective from what my husband does to how I am to love:

Refined Christian Prenup:

> I commit to you and God to love, honor, and cherish you until death parts us. As a sinner, if I lose my way and divorce you without biblical grounds or cheat on you, I will relinquish property rights and provide for you until death.

Ultimately, the difference between the secular prenup and the Christian prenup is the difference between self-centeredness and selflessness. Satan's goal is for us to focus on ourselves. There is no one-flesh doctrine, no trust, and no commitment. His goal is for you to be alone. God's goal is for us to become one with Him and with our spouses, trusting Him and committing to love until death. Satan's plan leads to destruction. God's plan leads to abundant life.

Blessing

May God grant you the wisdom to discover the peace and the beauty of the selfless life.

THE CHRISTIAN PRENUPTIAL AGREEMENT

The Power of the Prenup

Your prenup has the ability to release an amazing power and energy into your marriage. While others may wander into marriage hoping or expecting that everything will work out, your prenup empowers you to boldly enter marriage with an assurance that comes with seeking God's wisdom, gaining relevant knowledge, and then using this wisdom and knowledge to create a God-honoring plan. Preparing your prenup empowers you in thirteen specific areas.

1. The Power To Overcome the Dangers of "Attraction Love Drugs"

* * * * *

Love is a grave mental disease. — Plato

* * * * *

How could Plato be right when love feels so good? Cupid draws back his bow and takes aim right at your heart. You have been struck with the arrow of romantic love. You recognize it by the tingles in your toes, the sweat on your palms, the racing of your heart, and the fireworks that explode when your betrothed walks into the room. Everything seems new. All things are possible. You find yourself doing things that you never thought you would. You throw caution to the wind and race off into the sunset.

* * * * *

Does that "in love" feeling make you feel like someone disconnected your brain?
Do you care about anything other than your sweetheart?
Do you have a hard time focusing on work and serious matters?

* * * * *

God created us for relationship. As such, He created our bodies to produce various "love drugs" that cause two responses: attraction and attachment. These "love drugs" are actually neurochemicals that the body releases when we are attracted to another person. (See "The Chemistry of Love" in the Appendix for more details on the science behind neurochemicals.) The brain responds to these neurochemicals in similar ways as it does to certain narcotics, creating feelings of euphoria like being high. These chemicals are also highly addictive.

"Eros" Love

God created certain neurochemicals to drive us into serious relationships. These attraction chemicals lead to "eros" love, otherwise known as romantic love or infatuation. *Eros* is the Greek word for the kind of love that is conditioned on feelings. Our romantic feelings tell us that our love will always last. As long as our feelings are positive, we will stay in the relationship. However, unless you have built a deeper relationship, the smallest relational infraction could turn your feelings from romance to indifference or even bitterness. Building a relationship on feelings is like building a house on sand. If the sand shifts — as our emotions often do — then the house tumbles down.

Eros is a wonderful gift from God. It energizes and thrills us, but it's not meant to be the foundation of our marriage.

"Agape" Love

"Agape" is the Greek word that the Bible uses to describe the love God has for us. It is unconditional and is not based on feelings. It's the kind of love that is formed by actions and choosing to love, even when you don't feel like your spouse deserves it. The Bible tells us:

> *"This is real love — not that we loved God, but that he loved us and sent his Son as a sacrifice to take away our sins ... We love each other because he loved us first"* (1 John 4:10, 19, NLT).

God created our bodies to produce bonding neurochemicals that cause us to want to stay in relationship and give us a desire to be monogamous. These love drugs are what drive us to love the way that God loves us. Sometimes it's not easy, but with God's help and the bonding chemicals that He gives us, we have all the help that we need. *Agape* love is what's needed to get you to your 50th anniversary and help you fulfill your vision for a marital homerun.

Danger: Attraction Love Drugs Wear Off

* * * * *

Marriage is like a phone call in the middle of the night.
First there is the ring, and then you wake up.

* * * * *

THE CHRISTIAN PRENUPTIAL AGREEMENT

If we stayed "high" on the attraction love drugs, we would never get anything done. God created our system to phase out the need for these attraction chemicals, and phase in our bonding chemicals, which lay the foundation for our marriage. The good news is that the effects of the attractions chemicals wear off in eighteen months to three years, at which time you will become rational and useful again. The bad news is that when they wear off, you may feel like you sobered up and now find yourself married.

Based on the chemical phase out of infatuation, it's no surprise that the highest incidence of divorce is about four to five years after marriage when attraction love drugs have worn off. Through understanding this phenomenon and God's plan for *agape* love, you have the power to craft a prenuptial agreement that will help you transition through the neurochemical changes and build a marriage on the foundation of *agape* love.

Love Is Blind

* * * * *

After a lengthy quarrel, a wife said to her husband, "You know, I was a fool when I married you."

The husband replied: "Yes, dear, but I was in love and didn't notice it."

* * * * *

Scientists from the University College London have discovered that that feelings of love cause a suppression of activity in the brain that controls critical thought. They found that romantic love produces reduced activity in the systems necessary for making critical social assessments and negative judgments.[8] When you consider that you are making decisions that impact your lives "until death do you part," this can have some serious implications. It's important to understand four common, but dangerous, attitudes that can develop as a result of this reduced critical thinking:

THE POWER OF THE PRENUP

- You don't feel like dealing with serious issues.

- You believe your feelings of love will get you through the tough times.

- You believe you can figure out your differences after you are married.

- You believe your fiancé will change after the wedding.

While you may not want to snap out of the euphoria that you are feeling, now is the time to deal with looming potential issues and differences. They will not work themselves out.

God created you as unique individuals. Some differences between you are complementary, making you a good team and giving your relationship balance. For example, commonly one person will be a saver and the other a spender. Preparing your prenup gives you the opportunity to explore how you will resolve your financial differences. Otherwise, if the spender spends the couple into debt, the saver will harbor resentment. Similarly, if the saver keeps such tight reins on the money that the spender never has any disposable cash, the spender will harbor resentment.

While going through the process of preparing your prenup, you may find that you cannot reconcile important differences. In these cases, you may decide to either postpone or call off the wedding. Certain issues should be deal breakers. For example, Christians should not marry non-Christians in hopes that they will change after the wedding. Addictive behaviors or other behavioral issues should also be deal breakers.

The most dangerous attitude you can have before marriage is expecting that someone will change once you are married. If they have not changed before the wedding when the love drugs are flowing and their incentive to change is the highest, why would they change after the wedding?

THE CHRISTIAN PRENUPTIAL AGREEMENT

Your prenup gives you the power to overcome the suppression of critical thinking by helping you to take an objective look at your differences. While the love drugs are coursing through your veins, calling off or putting off the wedding may seem impossible, especially when you consider that your fiancé is essentially your love drug dealer. But there is great wisdom in being absolutely sure that it is the right time and you are marrying the right person. There is an old saying that goes, "Marriage is grand, but divorce is a hundred grand." The financial cost pales in comparison to the emotional devastation left in the wake of divorce. You can always decide to marry later — no harm done. But you cannot undo a marriage.

The process of preparing the prenuptial agreement brings you back to reality from the dreamy state of *eros*. It forces you back to sobriety as you make decisions about your plans and work to reconcile your differences. The prenuptial agreement is your most effective tool for overcoming the power of the *eros* love drugs. Do not underestimate their effects.

2. The Power To Overcome the Distraction of Wedding Planning

Wedding planning tends to demand every minute of your pre-wedding time and energy as you create the most beautiful wedding possible. Add this busy-ness to the drug-induced euphoria of love, and it may seem impossible to focus on the serious issues raised when you work on your prenup. The reality is that your wedding events only last a day or two, but your marriage lasts a lifetime. Shouldn't you spend at least as much time planning your marriage as planning your wedding?

Neither your *Pinterest* portfolio nor your wedding ceremony builds a foundation for marriage. But your prenup will. Spending the time to prepare your prenup will carry you through the good times and the bad. Keep the wedding planning in check; otherwise it may distract you from dealing with what is important — building your foundation.

3. The Power of a Plan and a Purpose

* * * * *

By failing to prepare, you are preparing to fail.
— Benjamin Franklin

* * * * *

Often our default goal for marriage is just getting there. *I want to be married.* Is your goal just to achieve a state of being, or do you have specific goals for your marriage? What do you want your obituary to say after you have gone on to Heaven? Will it say that you simply existed or that you accomplished x, y, and z? What do you want your lives and your marriage to count for?

Your prenuptial agreement is your opportunity to take the gift that God is giving you and make a plan for how to invest it. When Jesus was describing the costs to be a disciple, He described it this way:

> *"Suppose one of you wants to build a tower. Won't you first sit down and estimate the cost to see if you have enough money to complete it? For if you lay the foundation and are not able to finish it, everyone who sees it will ridicule you, saying, 'This person began to build and wasn't able to finish'"* (Luke 14:28-30).

Finishing well should be our goal. We look forward to a life filled with love, accomplishments, family, and ultimately, sitting on the veranda in rocking chairs with our grandchildren running around looking back on fifty great years of marriage. Are you ready to finish well? That's the power of planning and purpose.

 Take a few minutes to do the Preparation Exercise 2: "What Will Your Lives Count For?" Compare it to what you wrote about your marital homerun in Chapter 1.

THE CHRISTIAN PRENUPTIAL AGREEMENT

4. The Power of the Written Word

There is a power in the written word that does not exist with oral statements. One of the most common excuses I hear for divorce is: "We grew apart." I find this interesting, because most people vow to love one another until death parts them. What does growing apart have to do with the action of loving? When I ask what vows they took, they get a deer-in-the-headlights look implying, "Vows? What vows?" It's as if their oral agreements (vows) were meaningless.

In fact, Dr. Robin L. Smith wrote a secular book called *Lies at the Altar* that acknowledges that people will say a lot of things during their wedding ceremony that they have not thought through. They don't mean to lie, but they do not understand the depth and cost of the commitment that they are making.

Interestingly, when we put promises in writing, they become real. Perhaps this story will bring that home:

> One Friday night, I got a call from the mother of one of my son's friends. Somehow, Philip had gotten their car stuck in the middle of the vacant lot adjacent to the school's football field. They had to have it towed.
>
> There were two girls in the car when this incident occurred. My son swore he did not remember their names because they were new to his school. My lie detector went off. But even with grounding and prodding, he would not change his oral testimony.
>
> I secretly found out from the mother that one of the girls was the daughter of the dean of students who was not allowed to date because her father believed she was too young. Philip had already been in trouble for trying to date her. If her dad had found out about this incident, heads would have rolled.
>
> Sunday night, I wrote out Philip's account of the events, including a declaration that he did not know the names of those girls. Further, if his story were found to be untrue, then his car would be sold immediately, not to be replaced. I asked him to sign it.
>
> As Philip sat at the table, staring at the written words, beads of perspiration broke out on his forehead. Minutes seemed like

42

THE POWER OF THE PRENUP

hours as he stared at that document with a pen in his hand. Finally, he put the pen down and said he was ready to tell the truth. He proceeded to confess her identity.

What is it about writing those spoken declarations that forced his confession? What was it about being in writing that his words became real or had real consequences?

God had Moses, Solomon, and the other writers of the Bible write the history, the law, the wisdom, and the prophecy down for a reason. God knows that the written word cannot be changed or denied. He wanted a witness to His covenants with us so that we could be sure where we stood with Him. It gives us assurance of our salvation and a guide for our lives. It's a gift.

Similarly, the written prenup benefits couples in the following ways:

1. It confirms that we are entering into a covenant with each other.

2. It clarifies and confirms the vows that we are taking and the promises we are making.

3. It helps us take to heart the agreement we are making.

4. It can be revisited throughout the marriage as a reminder of what was promised.

5. It can be revisited throughout the marriage and amended as life changes so that you stay on the same page and don't grow apart.

6. It can be a legacy for your children to witness and possibly emulate when they are approaching their own marriages.

(For more on this topic, see "As It Is Written, so Shall It Be Done" in the Appendix.)

43

THE CHRISTIAN PRENUPTIAL AGREEMENT

5. The Power To Recognize the Sinful Nature of Man

One of the most important things to understand before you marry is that two sinners are marrying. While the chemicals of love are suppressing our critical thinking abilities, it is difficult, if not impossible, to see the faults of our intendeds. Even if we see their faults, we minimize or ignore the potential impact of those faults. But when the chemicals wear off, those faults become all too real. Furthermore, we put our best foot forward when we are dating, doing our best to hide our flaws from our fiancé. After the wedding, our old sin nature rears up, and we tend to head back to self-centeredness. This is not a modern phenomenon. It started in the Garden of Eden when Eve wanted more than what God provided.

Do you believe that man is basically good, especially your fiancé and, moreover, yourself? God tells us: *Indeed, there is no one on earth who is righteous, no one who does what is right and never sins (Ecclesiastes 7:20),* One of my favorite pastors once said, "We are all at any moment only one thought from a fall." That could take the form of alcoholism, drug abuse, gambling, pornography, adultery, violence, or just plain giving up. The consequences could be financial ruin, incapacity, death, or divorce.

The apostle Paul confessed his own sin nature like this:

> *I do not understand what I do. For what I want to do I do not do, but what I hate I do. And if I do what I do not want to do, I agree that the law is good. As it is, it is no longer I myself who do it, but it is sin living in me. For I know that good itself does not dwell in me, that is, in my sinful nature. For I have the desire to do what is good, but I cannot carry it out. For I do not do the good I want to do, but the evil I do not want to do — this I keep on doing. Now if I do what I do not want to do, it is no longer I who do it, but it is sin living in me that does it.*
>
> *So I find this law at work: Although I want to do good, evil is right there with me. For in my inner being I delight in God's law; but I see another law at work in me, waging war*

against the law of my mind and making me a prisoner of the law of sin at work within me. What a wretched man I am! Who will rescue me from this body that is subject to death? Thanks be to God, who delivers me through Jesus Christ our Lord! (Romans 7:15-25a).

Your prenup presents an opportunity to recognize that you are both sinners and to make a plan for how to deal with your sin nature when it starts to attack your marriage. It's like planning for and practicing a fire drill in school. Kids are taught to recognize the fire bell, and are taught how to exit the building in an orderly fashion. Because of this, there is no panic and there is a greater chance everyone will survive. Without a plan, there is no telling how people will react.

Take a moment to do Preparation Exercise 3: "Rules of Engagement."

The same applies to marriage. Having a plan to recognize when marriage gets out of balance and then knowing how to react will help keep your marriage stable and keep it from derailing when our sin nature strikes. When you are not getting your way or you don't feel loved, what will you do? What plans will you put into place to avoid divorce? How will you safely avoid the fire?

6. The Power To Remind Us Whom We Trust

One of the most common objections to prenups is that they imply a lack of trust. That is indeed true for a *secular* prenup, but if we truly grasp the depravity of man, should we trust our fiancé?

Without God and a view to eternity, unbelievers should put a secular plan in place for divorce. Our self-centered culture believes in a doctrine of "every man for himself" and "the one with the

THE CHRISTIAN PRENUPTIAL AGREEMENT

most toys wins." The world finds its solace in things and stores up its treasures in the temporal world. Compounded with our propensity to view everything that quits working or becomes boring as disposable, why should we trust our spouses to stick it out when things aren't going their way?

God does not intend for us to seek worldly shelter, either in the form of reliance on another, or reliance on our own resources. He intends for us to rely solely on Him. A *secular* prenup demonstrates a lack of trust in God's provision.

> *The* LORD *is my light and my salvation — whom shall I fear? The* LORD *is the stronghold of my life — of whom shall I be afraid? (Psalm 27:1).*

If you are honest with yourself, you recognize that you regularly fail in your own sin life. Because of man's sin nature, none of us truly deserve our spouse's trust. Your fiancé is entrusting you with his/her heart. What are you going to do to protect your fiancé from the effects of your sin nature?

Emotions and circumstances change, but God remains steadfast. Our trust should be fully placed in Christ. Our hope is not in the things of this earth (including our spouses), but in what Christ did for us on the cross. These lyrics from "My Hope Is Built" say it all:

> My hope is built on nothing less
> Than Jesus Christ, my righteousness;
> I dare not trust the sweetest frame,
> But wholly lean on Jesus' name.
>
> [Refrain]
> On Christ, the solid Rock, I stand;
> All other ground is sinking sand,
> All other ground is sinking sand.[9]

Your prenup has the power to remind you that no matter what is happening in your married life, God is in control. He has a plan and you can trust in that.

Whom do you trust?

 Take some time to do the Preparation Exercise 4: "Writing Your Statement of Faith."

7. The Power To Remind Us of True Property Rights

"It's mine!" That's the battle cry that reverberates whenever two children play together. Children in the back seat of a car on vacation draw an imaginary boundary line between them and, if it's crossed, they scream, "He's on my side!"

We never really get over that. When we go to the beach, we stake a territorial claim by laying a blanket down. We glare at strangers who get too close, giving them a look that says, *Don't you dare kick sand on my space or get too close. It's mine!*

Marriage is no exception. We claim special rights to our things: chairs, remote controls, drawer and closet space, garages, kitchens, and/or computers. We may not proclaim it like a two-year-old, but the heart cries, *It's mine!* For my divorce clients, it sounds more like, "I worked hard for that. It's mine, and I want it." (Of course, whatever one divorce client really wants, the other claims just for spite — and that pretty much takes us back to the two-year-old status.)

As adults, we spend much time and energy acquiring, defining, and defending property rights. The preponderance of the time and energy spent in courts by our legal community is focused on these rights. These rights are also the focus of most secular prenups. Even the Ten Commandments deals with property rights and the problems associated with them:

THE CHRISTIAN PRENUPTIAL AGREEMENT

"You shall have no other gods before me" (Exodus 20:3).

"You shall not steal" (Exodus 20:15).

"You shall not covet your neighbor's house. You shall not covet your neighbor's wife, or his male or female servant, his ox or donkey, or anything that belongs to your neighbor" (Exodus 20:17).

The first is included because stuff often becomes our God. In these passages, God does indicate that there is some entitlement to the use of property. But who does God say truly owns the property and how are we to view our rights to it?

- When He created the world, there was no mention of giving Adam and Eve land or any possessions. He gave them the right to receive the fruits of the land that He Himself had planted. (See Genesis 2.)

- *The earth is the Lord's, and everything in it, the world, and all who live in it (Psalm 24:1).*

- *"The land must not be sold permanently, because the land is mine [God's] and you reside in my land as foreigners and strangers" (Leviticus 25:23).*

- *"The silver is mine and the gold is mine," declares the Lord Almighty (Haggai 2:8).*

- *Do you not know that your bodies are temples of the Holy Spirit, who is in you, whom you have received from God? You are not your own; you were bought at a price. Therefore honor God with your bodies (1 Corinthians 6:19-20).*

- *For from him and through him and for him are all things (Romans 11:36a).*

THE POWER OF THE PRENUP

He calls us to be good stewards of the property with which He entrusts us. What kind of property planning honors God? Your prenup has the power to glorify God in how you acknowledge Him with regards to your property and how you provide for your spouse.

8. The Power To Avoid Entitleitis

Urban Dictionary defines "entitleitis" as: "Infectious thinking that one has an inherent right to something(s) by mere existence."[10] This disease is running rampant in our culture. Many people believe that they are entitled to receive things such as education, social status, cars, cell phones, etc. What do you believe you are entitled to receive from your spouse — in your marriage or as a lifestyle?

Your expectations are learned. Did you learn them from your parents, your friends, or the media? It is important to identify what you feel entitled to and where your expectations come from so that you don't get disappointed when your spouse does not provide you with what you believe you are entitled to.

The Bible teaches that there is only one thing that we are entitled to, and it's not riches or being pampered. *For the wages of sin is death, but the gift of God is eternal life in Christ Jesus our Lord (Romans 6:23).* Your prenup gives you the power to identify entitleitis — to recognize what you really deserve (death) and to set realistic expectations so that your marriage is not derailed when you do not get what you think you deserve.

9. The Power To Avoid Financial Stress

The average college student graduates college with $28,000 in student loan debt. They are also likely to have $5,000 in credit card debt. [11] Multiply that by two engaged graduates, and you would have $66,000 in debt as a wedding present. If your interest rate is

THE CHRISTIAN PRENUPTIAL AGREEMENT

4% and you want to pay it off in five years, that's a payment of about $1,200.00 per month.

Now suppose you want to buy a house that costs $200,000 fully financed at 5% interest payable over 30 years. Your mortgage payment would be just over $1,000.00 per month. Apartment rent would likely be about the same if not more. Your total monthly net is $2,200 before paying your tithe, real estate taxes, insurance, car payments, food costs, and a host of other living expenses. Is it any wonder that couples feel the pressure that both the husband and wife must work in order to make ends meet?

The Center for Marriage and Family at Creighton University studied couples during the first five years of their marriage. They ranked the top problems that couples under the age of 29 listed as stressing their marriages in this order:

1. Balancing job and family

2. Frequency of — or satisfaction with — sexual relations

3. Debt brought into the marriage (money)

4. Husband's employment (money)

5. Financial situation (money)

6. Expectations about household chores[12]

Notice that money is directly related to three of the top five. However, the reality is that because women are working, all six are related to finances. When women work, they feel stressed about #1. A tired woman (who is trying to balance job and family) may not be up to sex because she has spent all her energy on #1, which explains #2. A tired woman who is trying to do #1 and #2 may have higher expectations about sharing household chores, which leads to #6.

THE POWER OF THE PRENUP

Debt is a master. It diminishes your ability to make financial decisions unhindered. It often leads to resentment (#3), whether spoken or unspoken.

> *"No one can serve two masters. Either you will hate the one and love the other, or you will be devoted to the one and despise the other. You cannot serve both God and money"* (Luke 16:13).

Debt is often a sign of the inability to delay gratification. "I want it now; I'll pay for it later." If you cannot afford it today, how will you be able to afford it later when you have new needs or desires? And sadly, you may not even still have or be enjoying what you are still paying for.

One of the number one indicators of marital success is self-control, which is also one of the fruit of the Spirit (Galatians 5:22-23). Fifty years ago, Stanford University studied the effects of delayed gratification. They put pre-school children individually in a room with a single marshmallow on a plate in front of them. They told them that if they did not eat the marshmallow when the adult left the room, they would get two when the adult returned. The video of the experiment is precious. Interestingly, they did a longitudinal study later to discover how the children had fared in their adult lives. Those who had great self-control — those who did not eat the marshmallow — had much higher success rates in life.[13]

While traveling in Greece, we hired a taxi to take us to a point of interest. We asked our driver (an attractive 30ish man) if he was married. He said that he was holding off on marriage until he had enough saved to properly care for a wife, which included having an olive farm sufficient to support his future wife and family. While I am not recommending that couples wait until they have enough (because that may never happen), he was exhibiting great self-control and an attitude of self-sacrifice.

Your prenup has the ability to help you minimize financial stresses that could otherwise be deadly to your marriage. By planning how to avoid and eliminate debt, as well as budget for your future together, you can get control of your finances before you get into trouble.

To do this effectively, I recommend that you:

1. Complete the Preparation Exercise 5: "Financial Planning."

2. Exchange your financial documents.

3. Go through a personal financial class together to help you to understand budgeting and prioritizing cash flows. This may be one of the best investments of time and money that you can make. Check with your church or websites such as Crown Financial Ministries' website (www.crown.org) or Dave Ramsey's website (www.daveramsey.com) to find classes near you.

10. *The Power To Provide for Our Spouse in the Event We Fail*

Too often we view prenups as how we will protect ourselves if our spouse fails us. However, if we truly understand our sin nature, we must recognize that we have the potential to seemingly lose our minds and fall into sin. Every day, well-meaning Christians make mistakes such as confiding in someone of the opposite sex when things are not going well at home. Confiding leads to emotional attachments and a slippery slope to adultery.

People have been unfaithful to God since the Garden of Eden. People have always sought more out of life than what God has provided. God has always been faithful to His commitment to us regardless of our unfaithfulness to Him. Whether unfaithfulness takes the form of adultery or not living up to our vows to love our spouses, we will fail our spouses on some level.

THE POWER OF THE PRENUP

Do these failures mean that we divorce when we fail? God hates divorce. He never commands it, but rather allows for it because He knows that we are weak. He specifically allows for divorce in two instances, one of which is adultery. What will you do to avoid adultery? What will you do in the event of adultery? Your prenup is the opportunity to plan for this potential fire hazard.

Your Christian prenup gives you the opportunity to reflect the selflessness that God calls you to have toward your spouse. It should not be about what will happen if you give up; but rather, what will you do in the event *you* sin against your spouse? How will you provide for them? You promised to love, honor, and cherish until death. Your prenup gives you the power to provide for your spouse in the event *you* fall.

11. The Power To Protect the Godly Roles of Father and Mother

God reveres fatherhood and motherhood. He assigned men to be providers and protectors with a built-in need to be respected. He created women to be nurturers with a built-in need to be loved. Studies show that children who have stay-at-home moms are more likely to succeed in school and have fewer juvenile problems.[14] Unfortunately, our modern society does not have a reverence for these roles, which in turns undermines our abilities to feel as if our needs are being met (men for respect and women for love). For children, this means that they are going to struggle more to make their way in life.

The position of fathers in the family is mocked by media. Men in television sit-coms and movies are often made to appear as bumbling cavemen who are incapable of parenting. It is almost as if men have to think and behave like women to be seen as competent. Long gone are the days of *Father Knows Best.*

Men are also being supplanted in the workforce by women who are graduating from college and becoming professionals in greater numbers than men. Elementary and secondary schools are teaching

THE CHRISTIAN PRENUPTIAL AGREEMENT

using methods which cater to women's learning styles. Thus women are gaining an advantage in our school systems, leaving men with fewer opportunities to become the revered provider, and thus less likely to feel respected.

The image of motherhood has a different problem. Media portrays successful women as those who work outside the home. Gone are the days revering the role of homemaker/nurturer of June Cleaver from "Leave it to Beaver." Even parents encourage their daughters to go to work and keep their professions after they give birth to their children in case their marriages (or husbands) fail. Women are now more stressed and overworked because they attempt to do it all and be all. (This goes back to the study in #4 above.) They beat themselves up when they can't get it all done.[15]

Even when couples agree that husbands will be provider/protectors and wives will be nurturers, life may throw a curveball, such as disability, job loss, or divorce. How will that affect the couple's ability to fulfill their God-given roles as mothers and fathers?

Divorce, and the laws associated with it, has serious detrimental impact on children. While Satan whispers that the children are resilient, study after study proves that the outcomes for children of divorce are worse than for those who are raised in intact healthy homes. (See "What is Divorce and Family Fragmentation Costing You?" in the Appendix).

In Florida, child support guidelines are designed to calculate child support based upon both spouses working. Even if the mother has never worked, income will be "imputed" to her as if she were working, and the resulting child support will be reduced accordingly. In essence, the law effectively forces women who were committed to staying home to raise and nurture their families back to work.

Additionally, children are forced into timesharing schedules imposed by the courts (unless agreed to by the parties). As a result of child support being tied to number of "overnights" with each parent, it is common for fathers to seek equal time with the children, if for no other reason than to reduce their child support

THE POWER OF THE PRENUP

payments. Children have to learn to live in two homes on a schedule that could be two nights here, two nights there and rotating weekends. I don't know about you, but that would make me neurotic. I need stability to function. What's worse is that recent studies have shown that time-sharing for very young children causes serious separation problems.[16] What are we as a society doing to our kids?

Another problem is that divorced parents often use their children as weapons against their former spouses or as spies in their homes. Parents also often make the mistake of treating their children as little adults, sharing adult problems with them that they may otherwise have shared with their spouses. Further, parents often trash the other parent or otherwise try to alienate their children from their former spouses. This undermines honoring parents as God commands in Exodus 20:12.

Your prenup has the power to protect the roles of fatherhood and motherhood by remembering that God is the One who creates parents. Thus it is important to make provisions to honor God's choice and encourage godly roles. Even in the event of divorce, a couple can make plans that will attempt to honor God's plans to the greatest extent possible. This may include providing for the wife to stay home to raise the children. It may also include a promise by the mother to train the children to honor their father and help to nurture the father/child relationship in a way that honors the Lord.

12. The Power To Preserve Children's Inheritance

Couples who have children from previous relationships may desire to allocate some special inheritance for those children. For example, there may be an asset that has special meaning to that family such as a family portrait or collection that has been in the family for generations. The prenup has the power to carve out special property, not as an exclusion of property from a spouse, but as a gift to a child.

55

THE CHRISTIAN PRENUPTIAL AGREEMENT

13. *The Power To Overcome Satan's Attacks*

Marriage was the first institution that God ordained. God brings forth His righteous fruit through it. What better way for Satan to render us ineffective for the work of the Kingdom than to attack marriage? The Bible reminds us:

> *Be alert and of sober mind. Your enemy the devil prowls around like a roaring lion looking for someone to devour. Resist him, standing firm in the faith (1 Peter 5:8-9a).*

Satan's lies are subtle, often coming as whispers from the media or advice from well-meaning friends. What do his lies sound like? Perhaps something like this:

Satan: Yes, you need a prenup, but you don't need to waste time reading this book. What do you need to know about prenups, anyway? Just make a list of your stuff and get an attorney to draft it up. Relax. Love is all you need. Just focus on having the most beautiful wedding possible. The rest will take care of itself. You only get one chance to have the wedding you've always dreamed of.

Satan wants you to be distracted with your wedding and ignore the bigger issues. Do not be deceived. Be alert for his lies. They permeate our culture.

The best way to recognize counterfeit bills is to study and learn the characteristics of real bills. This book presents the real thing — God's truth. But the deceiver is clever. He presents God's truth with a twist, trying to confuse and give you reason to doubt God. If you are not vigilant, you may get suckered into bad thinking, which leads to pain and destruction. Jesus said:

> *"The thief comes only to steal and kill and destroy; I have come that they may have life, and have it to the full" (John 10:10).*

56

THE POWER OF THE PRENUP

Perhaps the best way to defend against his attacks is to recognize what makes him happy and design your prenup to counter his plans to defeat you. Satan is happy when:

- You get so enraptured with the wedding that you don't plan for your marriage. Your prenup helps you focus on what is important, which destroys his plan to distract you.

- You have a false sense of security based on your feelings. Your prenup keeps you from being lulled into a false sense of security by helping you focus on the realities of what you may face in marriage.

- You have no goals or plans for your life. If you don't know where you are going, it's easy for him to lead you astray. Your prenup helps you to set goals and make plans for how to achieve your goals and live a life that counts for eternity.

- One of you wins a fight, which means the other loses. If you become one flesh (as God designed), then a loss for one is a loss for both, and Satan wins. Your prenup gives you the power to anticipate conflict so neither of you is wounded in battle.

- You have unrealistic expectations for your spouse. The deceiver knows that your spouse is a mortal sinner. He will attack when you are disappointed with your spouse, and this could lead you to look elsewhere for what's missing. Your prenup has the power to help you set realistic expectations for each other so Satan cannot get a foothold.

- You get a "mine versus yours" mentality. He knows that a cord of three strands is hard to attack. When you are one with each other and with God, Satan cannot break in. When you separate into selfish mode, you are easy prey. Your prenup helps you focus on the unity of marriage.

THE CHRISTIAN PRENUPTIAL AGREEMENT

- The roles of men and women/fathers and mothers are blurred. Satan is the father of lies and the author of confusion. He attacks when our roles and goals are not clearly defined. The prenup gives you the power to recognize your God-given roles and to enjoy an abundant life.

Your prenup gives you the opportunity to thwart Satan's attempts to derail your marriage and is your greatest insurance policy against his attacks.

Blessing

May [God] give you the desire of your heart and make all your plans succeed.
May we shout for joy over your victory and lift up our banners in the name of our God.
May the LORD grant all your requests (Psalm 20:4-5).

5

Impact of Secular Law[17]

* * * * *

Do you, Adam, take Eve to be your lawfully wedded Wife?

* * * * *

Do you know what marriage means legally? When you take your vows and sign your marriage license, you are making commitments that have legal implications — both state and federal. Even without a prenup, but certainly before preparing one, it is important to have a basic understanding of legal matters. These are some of the basic legal implications of marriage:

- Your tax filing status will change.

- You can take title to property differently.

- You may be entitled to receive some or all of your spouse's property if he/she dies before you.

- You may become your spouse's medical surrogate.

THE CHRISTIAN PRENUPTIAL AGREEMENT

- Your income earned and property acquired will most likely be marital.

- You may have to pay alimony and give up property in the event of divorce.

- You may be entitled to a portion of your spouse's social security at retirement.

- You may not have to testify against your spouse, either civilly or criminally, in the event of a legal action against them.

Each state has unique laws related to marriage. It is therefore important that you learn how your state laws will impact you. Sometimes states appear to have similar laws, but case law or nuances can make them different. For example, all states have no-fault divorce laws, but some still have elements of fault that can affect the outcome of a divorce. Even the requirements for a legal marriage vary.

The purpose of this chapter is to help you understand issues that you need to address. Based on this information, you may decide to seek professional services for financial, estate, tax, or other legal planning. Consult with an attorney before making legal decisions.

1. Eligibility to Marry

Are you eligible to marry legally? States have different requirements that may include:

- Being a certain age, or, if under that required age, parental or judicial consent

IMPACT OF SECULAR LAW

- Having the capacity to marry — meaning being in the state of mind to understand marriage and not being otherwise emotionally or mentally incapacitated or coerced

- Having blood tests, proof of vaccinations, and/or good health

- Termination of previous marriages through death, divorce, or annulment

- Relational distance, such as not marrying a sibling or cousin

- Waiting periods between applying for a marriage license and the ceremony

- Licenses to marry

The federal government prohibits "sham marriages" — those conducted for the sole purpose of circumventing immigration laws. This was the basis for the movie, *The Proposal*, in which the character played by Sandra Bullock attempted to thwart her deportation by forcing her subordinate employee to marry her. These marriages are considered marriage fraud and perpetrators can face prison, a fine, or both.[18]

2. License to Marry

Are you already married in the eyes of the law? While traveling in Kansas, I met a young lady who was going through a divorce. She claimed that she did not know that she was married until she tried to leave her partner. They had lived together and had a child

THE CHRISTIAN PRENUPTIAL AGREEMENT

together. She was emphatic that she did not know she was married and was unhappy about what it was costing her to get divorced.

While most states require a license to marry, there are a number of states that have Common Law doctrines. In these states you may already be considered and/or declared married without the benefit of a marriage license or wedding ceremony.

Common Law marriages are generally non-ceremonial relationships that require "a positive mutual agreement, permanent and exclusive of all others, to enter into a marriage relationship, cohabitation sufficient to warrant a fulfillment of necessary relationship of man and wife, and an assumption of marital duties and obligations." [19] When Common Law marriages are challenged, most jurisdictions look to this three-prong test:

1. Agreement that you are married
2. Cohabitation
3. Public representations of marriage

Most states have repealed Common Law marriage doctrines and instead require a license for marriage. Once issued and solemnized by a duly authorized representative of the state, couples submit to their state's authority and the laws by which marriages are governed. However, there is a form of reciprocity where if you are deemed married by Common Law in one state and you move to a state that does not have Common Law marriages, you may be deemed married by function of the state in which you were married.

States generally require a solemnization ceremony for the marriage to be valid. The statutes dictate who can officiate. For example, the state may allow ordained ministers, notary publics, judges, or other officers of the court to solemnize marriages. Some jurisdictions require a license to perform the ceremony even if the person is an ordained minister. There is also generally a

IMPACT OF SECULAR LAW

requirement that a certain number of witnesses (at least two) be present.

While there are no specific words that must be said during the ceremony, generally the couple must verbally agree to take each other as husband and wife in the presence of the witnesses. Jurisdictions also generally require a pronouncement of marriage. Then the required parties (husband, wife, officiator, and witnesses) must sign the marriage license. Most couples are considered married when the ceremony ends, although the license must be signed and recorded as proof of marriage.

3. Consummation

Consummation is a word that indicates completion, usually used in context of a contract. A marriage is considered consummated after the couple takes their vows and has sexual intercourse. A few states have explicit requirements for the marriage to be consummated; otherwise, the marriage may be annulled. No state requires proof of consummation.

4. Covenant Marriage Laws

Christian marriage is a covenant with God and your spouse and not merely a contractual operation of law. From God's perspective, marriage paints a picture of His covenant relationship with us. The Bible proclaims the Church as the Bride of Christ. When a Christian accepts God's free gift of salvation, we enter a covenant relationship with Him. God's covenant relationship with us is one where He promises to save us, not based on our behavior, but rather on Christ's redemption.

Secular marriage laws generally do not reflect God's standard. All fifty states have adopted various forms of no-fault divorce that allow spouses to leave their marriage for "irreconcilable differences." As divorces have become easier to obtain and less of

THE CHRISTIAN PRENUPTIAL AGREEMENT

a stigma, divorce rates have continued to climb. Cultural media even promotes the idea that first marriages are training marriages, thereby indicating an expectation that divorce is inevitable — and even a good thing.

In reaction to this cultural shift and higher divorce rates, there has been a movement in some states to adopt covenant marriage laws. A legally recognized covenant marriage is one that requires three components: premarital counseling, marriage counseling if the marriage is having difficulties, and limited grounds for divorce such as domestic violence, adultery, or criminal activity. Louisiana, Arkansas, and Arizona are the only three states that currently offer covenant marriage licenses. However, similar laws have been proposed in over twenty states. Choosing this type of license is voluntary. Only 1-3% of couples have taken advantage of these licenses.

Oklahoma is currently one state that is considering Covenant Marriage laws. Oklahoma Senator Josh Brecheen, the promoter of this bill, explains his reason for putting this bill forward:

> The point of covenant marriage is not to make divorce impossible but to ensure that couples make every effort to reconcile when possible. We must do something to slow the growing rate of divorce in our state. According to statistics, divorce not only increases a state's poverty rate, but also inflicts psychological and social damage upon children that can be carried into adulthood.[20]

5. Name Changes

Women often take their husbands' names when they marry. This symbolizes becoming one flesh. A common tradition for marriage is to take or replace your middle name with your maiden name, and take your husband's name as a last name. Another popular idea is to hyphenate your maiden name with your husband's last name. This may be more important for a professional woman who has personal goodwill associated with her name.

To legally change your name, you must provide proof of marriage or name change to various governmental agencies, such as the driver's license bureaus, the Social Security Administration (SSA), and/or the Federal Passport Office. Often, this proof must be an original or certified copy of your marriage license, along with other identifying documentation, such as a passport or driver's license.

When you file your federal income tax return, you must file with the name that is recorded with SSA. Otherwise, your tax return will be rejected until such a time as you change your name on your tax return or with the Social Security Administration. To change your name with SSA, just log onto their website at www.ssa.gov and fill out the application for a new card. Either take or mail your application along with your identifying documentation as detailed on the website to the local office and you should receive your new card within ten business days.

Also note that if you travel abroad on your honeymoon, your travel documents must match your identification documents. Thus, if the couple is honeymooning immediately after the wedding, a bride will travel under her maiden name until she can return to have her driver's license and passport re-issued with her married name.

If you are opening joint accounts once married, you will handle the name recognition then. Otherwise, you will need to change your name on your existing separate accounts. This would also apply to any investment or retirement accounts that you might hold.

These are other places where you may need to change your name (once you have changed your name on your primary documents):

- Work (when you get your new social security card)
- Post office
- Utility company

THE CHRISTIAN PRENUPTIAL AGREEMENT

- Credit card companies
- Schools
- Landlord/mortgage companies
- Doctors' offices
- Insurance companies
- Voter registration
- Your attorney (to update legal documents, including your will)

6. Property Ownership

Most state laws recognize that property accumulated during the marriage is marital property. Most states' doctrines also establish that what you owned before marriage remains your individual property unless it is "transmuted" into marital property. Transmuting is the process of changing the character of the asset into a new character. For example, if upon marriage you add your spouse to your personal bank account, the ownership is transmuted from separate to marital property. This is considered an "intentional transmutation." However, assets could become considered marital unintentionally by changing the property itself (such as home improvements) or by comingling the assets acquired during marriage with the assets owned prior to marriage.

As Christians we are called to become one flesh in marriage, so there should not be a property distinction, because your property belongs to the new "you." Christian vows generally contain these words: "With this ring, I thee wed, and with all my worldly goods, I thee endow." A more accurate reflection of that statement would require you to re-title all your property to include your beloved on your wedding day.

Interestingly, property laws in certain states provide for a unique entity ownership for marriage. It's called "tenancy by the entireties." This term describes joint ownership in a manner more consistent with the one-flesh requirement found in Genesis 2:24. Essentially you both own 100% of the property and cannot

IMPACT OF SECULAR LAW

separately sell off a portion of the interest. This type of ownership interest can also provide protection against creditors who only have a cause of action against one spouse. For example, if you own your bank account in tenancy by the entireties and someone sues one of you because of a car accident, the judgment creditor may not be able to garnish the account.

7. Income Taxes

When you are single, you can file your taxes as either "single" or "head of household." Married taxpayers may generally file as either "married filing jointly" or "married filing separately." If a couple is separated, one or both may be able to file as "head of household" under certain circumstances. Filing jointly has historically yielded a more favorable tax result for most taxpayers.

The one-flesh doctrine is also evidenced in the tax code as it relates to ownership of businesses. If a husband or wife independently owns less than a controlling interest in a company, but in combination they own a controlling interest, then the IRS deems the ownership to be controlling, which may have implications on the tax treatment of the property.

8. Death and Inheritance

If someone dies without a will, they are considered to have died "intestate." Dying intestate usually requires a legal process called "probate," in which the court settles the estate. This can be costly and time consuming. Without a will, assets owned by a deceased single person free of debt usually go first to children (if they have any) or back up the family tree to parents, grandparents, etc. Once married, spouses generally inherit some, if not all, of the intestate decedent's assets.

Even with a will, some states do not allow one spouse to totally cut the other spouse completely out of the estate. The state makes

THE CHRISTIAN PRENUPTIAL AGREEMENT

provisions for the spouse to get some portion. For example, in Florida the minimum that a spouse will receive as of the date of this writing is thirty percent of the estate.

When designating a beneficiary for IRAs or other retirement plans, if you choose to name someone other than your spouse, your spouse must generally sign a waiver acknowledging that they are accepting your choice. If you already own retirement plans when you get married, it is important to update them with your spouse's name or get a waiver from your spouse if you have chosen another party.

9. Estate Taxes

Estate taxes provide special treatment for married couples. Tax law generally allows a widow/widower to inherit their deceased spouse's estate tax free. Special trusts can be set up to exclude a certain amount of taxes from income tax for inheritance purposes for the benefit of the heirs. You should consult with an estate attorney regarding these matters.

10. Social Security

Once married, you may be entitled to Social Security based on your spouse's earnings record. For example, when the husband of a stay-at-home mom retires, his wife may be eligible to receive an amount of social security based upon her husband's earnings. This does not detract from his payments while he is still alive, but she does not receive his full amount. In the event that he predeceases her, she would be entitled to his full amount.

If you both work, at retirement age there may be some planning involved regarding whose social security you should take. The social security website suggests the following:

IMPACT OF SECULAR LAW

If you have reached your full retirement age, and are eligible for a spouse's or ex-spouse's benefit *and* your own retirement benefit, you may choose to receive only spouse's benefits. If you do that, you can delay receiving your own retirement benefit until a later date to take advantage of delayed retirement credits.[21]

In the event of divorce, if you have been married for a number of years (currently at least ten years), then you may be able to keep your entitlement to collect based on your spouse's pay history, but there are restrictions. These rules are complex. There are exceptions and rules change, so it is important to familiarize yourself with the rules so that when you retire, you maximize your social security benefits.

11. Disability

Health care surrogates are people who dictate how medical treatment is to be administered to an incapacitated person. Unless otherwise documented, parents of singles and spouses of marrieds are generally the default surrogates.

There was a highly publicized case in the news about a woman, Terri Schiavo, who was in a vegetative state for fifteen years. Her husband wanted to take her off life support stating that she would not have wanted to remain alive artificially. Her parents objected. Her husband eventually prevailed.

You can legally appoint another if you do not like the default mode for your state's laws. As such, it is important to determine your state laws and to understand who your health care surrogate would be.

THE CHRISTIAN PRENUPTIAL AGREEMENT

12. Divorce

No one wants to believe divorce is a possibility, especially romantically-charged Christians who profess to be committed to the Lord. Unfortunately, no-fault divorce provisions mean that, while it takes two to tango, it only takes one to quit. There are a number of states that have both fault and no-fault options, the difference is whether you want to wait through the statutory separation period, which can be up to five years (Idaho) if contested. In those states, the best you can do to attempt to save your marriage legally is to slow the divorce down, with a hope for changed hearts and minds.

No-Fault Doctrine

Until the mid-1900s, courts granted divorces based on statutory "grounds" for dissolution. These grounds for divorce included abuse, cruelty, desertion, adultery, imprisonment, alcohol/drug addiction, insanity, and inability to perform sexual intercourse (if this was not disclosed prior to the marriage). The complaining spouse had to prove grounds existed in court.

No-fault law advocates claimed that trying to prove the grounds led to much courtroom drama that was sometimes trumped up. In order to remove the acrimony from divorce, states implemented "no-fault" divorce laws. One of the first states to do this was California. In 1969, then Governor Ronald Reagan signed the no-fault divorce provision into law. His son, Michael Reagan, in his book *Twice Adopted*, wrote this, "Dad later said that he regretted signing the no-fault divorce bill and [said] that he believed it was one of the worst mistakes he ever made in office."[22]

One of the greatest surprises to me when I began working in this field was that there were no punitive damages to parties when they did not uphold their end of marital "contracts." After all, when a couple marries, there are elements of a contract: offer (proposal), acceptance ("yes," followed by a license and solemnizing ceremony), consideration (a ring), with a promise to perform (love,

70

IMPACT OF SECULAR LAW

honor, cherish), and to do so for a specified time (until death). Contract law holds that parties should be held accountable to perform as agreed. When one party fails to perform, courts may award compensatory damages to the injured party. Imagine how businesses would be impacted if courts treated other contract law the way they treat marriage law. If there were no consequences for failure to perform, contracts would be meaningless.

No-fault divorce means that there may be no damages awarded to the offended spouse by the one breaking the covenant. For the purposes of splitting up the marital estate or the award of alimony, the fact that one party committed adultery will most likely not be a factor in the allocation of the estate or support. There may be a recovery by the offended spouse if the offender wasted marital assets on an extra-marital affair, and the offended party can document that spending. Sadly, the burden of proof is usually on the offended spouse. Such proof is often difficult and costly to obtain.

The no-fault doctrine can seem unfair in two ways. In a short-term marriage, an adulterer may walk away with little or no cost or consequences. In a long-term marriage, a non-working adulterer may be awarded alimony from the innocent spouse for life. However, as Christians, we should never lose sight of the fact that the seemingly "innocent" spouse has contributed to the decline of the marriage in some way. Furthermore, we must remember that "fairness" is not the Christian standard. It was not fair that Jesus had to pay my sin penalty.

The bottom line is that marriage takes two committed partners who agree to stick it out in very intentional ways. Perhaps it is more surprising that, because of our sin nature and propensity for demanding "fairness," more marriages don't fail.

Division of Property

When couples divorce, someone has to determine how the property will be divided. The couple may agree to a division that does not require legal intervention or, if they cannot agree, then a

THE CHRISTIAN PRENUPTIAL AGREEMENT

judge will decide. Judges rule based upon the law. There are generally two types of property and two ways to divide the property.

As we have already discussed, the two types of property are marital and non-marital. Marital property is considered jointly owned. Non-marital property is property that has been excluded from the marital estate and is considered separately owned.

There are two doctrines under which states operate for the division of property. Most states follow the equitable distribution doctrine, meaning that courts will divide marital property "equitably." Consequently, the marital property will generally be divided equally in terms of value, but specific property may be designated to one person or another. The judge may also give one spouse a disproportionate amount of the assets based upon the circumstances, which they deem makes the division more equitable.

The other doctrine is community property. Under this doctrine, the courts divide the property equally. This doctrine is generally found in the southwest United States.

Alimony

Alimony is a payment made by one spouse to provide support for their separated or divorced spouse. Generally it is made by the spouse who has been the provider in the marriage and is made to help maintain the former spouse's lifestyle or to avoid one spouse from being left destitute.

Prior to the 1960s, very few women worked outside the home and women were dependent on their husbands for support. Except in cases of infidelity, alimony was almost always awarded to a woman to make her "whole" financially. Today alimony may be awarded to either a man or woman. If awarded, it will most likely be based on the recipient's basic or lifestyle needs and the ability of the payor to pay.

In Florida, there are various forms of alimony: bridge-the-gap, rehabilitative, durational, and permanent. The first three may apply

IMPACT OF SECULAR LAW

when a marriage is shorter than seventeen years. "Bridge-the-gap" alimony is awarded to support a spouse for a brief time to help them financially acclimate back to single life. "Rehabilitative" alimony provides support for training or schooling so that the recipient can attain a certain profession or vocation. "Durational" alimony provides support for a period of time less than the term of the marriage. Of course, "permanent" alimony supports an ex-spouse until their death, remarriage, or entry into a substantively supportive relationship (a pseudo-marriage). Unless otherwise agreed upon, most forms of alimony can be modified if there are significant changes in the financial circumstances of either party. There is currently a movement underway in Florida to eliminate permanent alimony.

Children's Issues

Historically, courts awarded custody to mothers, as they were deemed to be the better nurturers. In more recent years, courts have been moving toward giving both parties equal time with the children, unless there is some evidence that shows one of the parties may not be emotionally or physically suitable to care for their children. States often employ a set of factors to determine how much time each parent will have with the children. In cases where there is an emotional instability issue, courts may order that the visitations should be supervised or denied altogether.

Adultery by one spouse does not prohibit children from staying with the adulterer, even if that spouse is sleeping with another person. Objectionable behavior, movies, or music (from a Christian perspective) does not generally impact custody issues, unless it is viewed as harmful to the children. Except for unsafe environments, there may be little you can do to restrict the environment that your child is exposed to when the child is with your ex-spouse. Having ministered to hundreds of single parents over the years, this seems to be one of the most heart-wrenching consequences of divorce.

Faith issues also arise in divorce. Suppose you have verbally agreed to raise your children as Christians, and your spouse

THE CHRISTIAN PRENUPTIAL AGREEMENT

becomes a Buddhist. There may be little that you can do to protect your children from non-Christian teaching if you have not recorded your desires in a prenuptial agreement. But beware that your prenup agreement on this issue is not a guarantee that your provision will hold up in court.

Courts can award child support regardless of marital status. Most states —with some variations among states — consider it a requirement of both parents to financially support children until they reach majority. Courts consider a number of factors, including the parents' income, the number of children, special needs, and whether there are children from previous relationships.

Providing for your children in the event of divorce is an area of your prenup that will take careful planning by you and your attorney.

Prior Marriages or Children from Prior Relationships

Prior marital settlement agreements, marital dissolution judgments, child support orders, and/or child custody orders generally take precedent over subsequent marriages and children. These orders may contain provisions for support payments to children of prior relationships or to prior spouses, property distributions that have not yet been settled, debt which has not yet been paid, and time-sharing issues with children.

It is important to review these documents with an attorney to understand how these prior relationships affect your upcoming marriage.

13. Enforceability of Prenups

Recognizing that jurisdictions may vary, there are certain elements generally required for enforceability, such as:

- **Disclosure:** There should be full and reasonable disclosure of the nature and extent of assets and liabilities

IMPACT OF SECULAR LAW

at the time of execution. It's a good idea to present each other with tax returns, brokerage and bank statements, documents related to debt, or any potential liabilities that may arise. Attach the financial disclosure to the agreement so that there is no question related to what was disclosed at a later date.

- **Independent Counsel:** Each party should have the opportunity to have their own attorney so that they understand the agreement and what they are giving up by entering into it. While not a requirement, it may also be good to have an accountant or financial advisor review the financial information to help explain its significance.

- **Voluntary:** Both parties should enter voluntarily and without coercion, duress, or overreaching. Timing may be critical, as those presented a few days prior to a wedding may be considered invalid due to duress. Pregnancy or immigration status may also be a factor in consideration of duress. Having your agreement ratified or videotaping the signing helps to demonstrate the voluntary nature of the agreement.

- **Not Unconscionable:** Terms should be fair with neither person being left in a harmful position. It is recommended to make sure that both people will be able to function financially after a divorce.

- **In writing:** Oral agreements are generally not enforceable.

- **Witnessed:** Generally, a notary public is required.

THE CHRISTIAN PRENUPTIAL AGREEMENT

14. Marriage Confidence Privilege

* * * * *

A grandmother overheard her 5-year-old granddaughter playing "wedding." The wedding vows went like this: "You have the right to remain silent, anything you say may be held against you, you have the right to have an attorney present. You may kiss the bride."[23]

* * * * *

Couples have a marriage confidence privilege that they can assert if one of them is asked to appear in court to testify against the other. By law, they do not have to if:

1. No one else was present when the confidential information was obtained; and,

2. Both agree that the information was confidential.

A spouse can assert the marital confidence privilege in civil and criminal court cases. It is not a requirement, but rather a privilege. The spouse may testify against their spouse if they want to.

15. Summary

Regardless of whether or not you choose to prepare a prenuptial agreement, I recommend that every couple consult with an attorney prior to marriage to understand the laws imposed by their state. The legal ramifications of marriage cannot be overemphasized.

IMPACT OF SECULAR LAW

Now that you have a broad overview of how secular laws may impact your marriage, we will now review God's laws and how they affect you.

Blessing

May God use this information to help you formulate a prenup that honors Him and nullifies or reduces the negative impact of counter-Christian marital laws.

THE CHRISTIAN PRENUPTIAL AGREEMENT

6

What Does God Want for You?

Power unleashed. Fireworks exploding. Space shuttles lifting off. There is nothing more exhilarating than the moment that power is unleashed. These power events are not just happenstance; they are the results of the scientific study of power, meticulous measurement, and careful planning. Lack of planning or tampering with the ingredients can yield dangerous outcomes.

Home Improvement was a television sitcom series produced during the 1990s starring Tim Allen who played "Tim the Tool Man Taylor," the host of a home improvement show. Tim was always seeking more power out of his tools. He would tweak his tools and appliances to get more power in ways that were never intended by the manufacturers. His enhancements always led to outcomes that, while humorous for entertainment purposes, were disastrous. (My favorite was the time he powered up the dishwasher and the back side of it exploded out into his kitchen.)

Just as manufacturers know the best and highest use for their products; God knows the greatest and best use for our marriages.

THE CHRISTIAN PRENUPTIAL AGREEMENT

Dearly beloved, we are gathered together here in the sight of God, and in the face of this congregation, to join together this Man and this Woman in holy Matrimony; which is an honorable estate, instituted of God in the time of man's innocency, signifying unto us the mystical union that is betwixt Christ and His Church; which holy estate Christ adorned and beautified with His presence, and first miracle that He wrought, in Cana of Galilee; and is commended of Saint Paul to be honourable among all men: and therefore is not by any to be enterprised, nor taken in hand, unadvisedly, lightly, or wantonly, to satisfy men's carnal lusts and appetites, like brute beasts that have no understanding; but reverently, discreetly, advisedly, soberly, and in the fear of God; duly considering the causes for which Matrimony was ordained.[24]

This chapter contains ten areas where God gives us instructions. If these instructions are incorporated into your marriage and your prenup, they will unleash great power into your marriage. Take the time to consider them reverently, discreetly, advisedly, soberly, and in the fear of God.

1. Leave the Nest

The first instruction that God gave us regarding marriage was that we are to leave our fathers and mothers. (See Genesis 2:24.) This is more than just physically moving out of the house. It means that you will transfer your allegiance from your parents to your spouse. It's almost like changing teams or gaining citizenship in a new country. Your job is now to protect and defend your new family.

In traditional marriage vows, we say, "forsaking all others." Most of us believe that means that we burn our "little black books" and no longer pursue relationships with the opposite sex. But it goes much deeper. It relates to reliance on anyone other than our spouse, which can be a problem if a bride or groom continues to seek their parents' advice over his or her spouse's.

For example, after their marriage, Suzie moved into Steve's house that had been decorated by Steve's mom. Steve would not let Suzie move anything or give the house her own touches because he did not want to offend his mother. Steve was not trying to be a jerk; he was trying to honor his mother, as we are commanded to do in Exodus 20:12.

What did Suzie do when they had a fight about this? She called her mom, told her what a jerk Steve was, and ran home to her parents' house. This is equally problematic. While parents serve as referees for their children's sibling rivalries, that is not their job in their children's marriages.

It is important to respectfully establish the new "you" when you marry. This can be difficult if Mom and Dad are not ready to let go. It can be more difficult when Mom and Dad are footing the bill for the wedding and they feel as though that gives them license to dictate certain aspects of your life. But it is important to do so.

Setting boundaries and forsaking all others is tough, but when done properly, you will reap a harvest of blessings from it.

(The Preparation Exercise 6: "Keeping In-Laws from becoming Out-Laws" provides practical tips to help with balancing leaving the nest with honoring your parents.)

2. Become "Us"

The LORD God said, "It is not good for the man to be alone. I will make a helper suitable for him."... So the LORD God caused the man to fall into a deep sleep; and while he was sleeping, he took one of the man's ribs and then closed up the place with flesh. Then the LORD God made a woman from the rib he had taken out of the man, and he brought her to the man.

THE CHRISTIAN PRENUPTIAL AGREEMENT

The man said, "This is now bone of my bones and flesh of my flesh; she shall be called 'woman,' for she was taken out of man."

That is why a man leaves his father and mother and is united to his wife, and they become one flesh (Genesis 2:18, 21-24).

Marriage is a unique state of being created by God. It is the state of "us." When Jesus described this union, He said: *"So they are no longer two, but one flesh. Therefore what God has joined together, let no one separate" (Matthew 19:6).* Older translations call the union "cleaving," which has wonderful connotations:

Cleave: to cling, stick, stay close, keep close, stick to, stick with, follow closely, join to, overtake, catch ... to stay with, to be joined together. [25]

The Hebrew word used in Genesis 2:24 to describe one flesh is "echad." It is the same word that God uses when He describes Himself as one (unity) in Deuteronomy 6:4: *Hear, O Israel: The LORD our God, the LORD is one.* The plural form of God, "Elohim," is used here indicating a plural God is one, supporting our Christian belief in the triune nature of God (Father, Son, and Holy Spirit). In the same way that our finite minds find it difficult to understand the mystical nature of the Trinity, so we struggle to understand mystical nature of "us."

Becoming one flesh is not just doctrine; it is a scientifically supported physiological phenomenon that occurs when a couple consummates their union. The body releases a chemical bonding agent called oxytocin, which, along with dopamine, acts as marital superglue. Oxytocin is also released when a woman nurses her baby, allowing the mother to bond with her baby. (For the other factors involved in this bonding, see "The Chemistry of Love" in the Appendix.)

WHAT DOES GOD WANT FOR YOU?

Secular prenuptial agreements are often written to keep property separate, which in essence deprives one spouse of property or income rights belonging to the other. Further, state laws often define premarital or inherited property as belonging separately to that spouse. By maintaining this "yours" and "mine" mentality, doesn't this inhibit or prevent the creation of "us"? Shouldn't the property that belongs to "us" be described as "ours"? Couldn't keeping property separate be considered self-serving and spouse-hating?

In this same way, husbands ought to love their wives as their own bodies. He who loves his wife loves himself. After all, no one ever hated their own body, but they feed and care for their body, just as Christ does the Church — for we are members of his body. "For this reason a man will leave his father and mother and be united to his wife, and the two will become one flesh." This is a profound mystery — but I am talking about Christ and the Church. However, each one of you also must love his wife as he loves himself, and the wife must respect her husband (Ephesians 5:28-33).

3. Great Sex

God created sex for married couples to enjoy, as is evidenced by these scriptures.

Enjoy life with your wife, whom you love, all the days of this meaningless life that God has given you under the sun — all your meaningless days. For this is your lot in life and in your toilsome labor under the sun (Ecclesiastes 9:9).

May your fountain be blessed, and may you rejoice in the wife of your youth (Proverbs 5:18).

83

THE CHRISTIAN PRENUPTIAL AGREEMENT

The Song of Solomon is an entire book of the Bible dedicated to passionate love-making. In fact, Hebrew boys were not allowed to study this book until they had gone through their bar mitzvah. Here is one passage.

How beautiful your sandaled feet, O prince's daughter!
Your graceful legs are like jewels, the work of an artist's
*   hands.*
Your navel is a rounded goblet that never lacks blended wine.
Your waist is a mound of wheat encircled by lilies.
Your breasts are like two fawns, like twin fawns of a gazelle.
Your neck is like an ivory tower.
Your eyes are the pools of Heshbon by the gate of Bath
*   Rabbim.*
Your nose is like the tower of Lebanon looking toward
*   Damascus.*
Your head crowns you like Mount Carmel.
Your hair is like royal tapestry; the king is held captive by its
*   tresses.*
How beautiful you are and how pleasing, my love, with your
*   delights!*
Your stature is like that of the palm, and your breasts like
*   clusters of fruit.*
I said, "I will climb the palm tree; I will take hold of its fruit."
May your breasts be like clusters of grapes on the vine, the
*   fragrance of your breath like apples, and your mouth like*
*   the best wine (Song of Songs 7:1-9a).*

Aside from the pleasurable aspect of love-making, research has also proven that sex within marriage is good for you and your relationship. As described in "The Chemistry of Love" in the Appendix, various neurochemicals are released during sex that promote bonding and monogamy. Furthermore, married couples who develop healthy and satisfying sex lives have fewer health problems, such as heart disease and depression.[26]

WHAT DOES GOD WANT FOR YOU?

Inasmuch as sex is one of the most anticipated benefits of marriage, our sexual relationships are often a source of problems. There are seasons where sexual intimacy is strained or out of balance. Sometimes, withholding sex is a weapon used against a spouse. It is imperative to find ways to get your sex life back on track. There are several great books on the subject, including: *Sexual Intimacy in Marriage* by William Cutrer and Sandra Glahn, *Intended for Pleasure* by Ed Wheat, and *A Blessing for the Heart: God's Beautiful Plan for Marital Intimacy* by James E. Sheridan.)

4. Fidelity

"Semper fi" is the motto of the U.S. Marine Corps. It is short for the Latin term, *semper fidelis*, which means "always faithful." God created us to be monogamous, having only one spouse and remaining faithful to him/her. There are two forms of not being faithful: fornication (having sex before marriage) and adultery (having sex outside of marriage).

> *"You shall not commit adultery" (Exodus 20:14).*

> *"You have heard that it was said, 'You shall not commit adultery.' But I tell you that anyone who looks at a woman lustfully has already committed adultery with her in his heart" (Matthew 5:27-28).*

The apostle Paul, when describing the qualifications for overseers, deacons, and elders, described faithfulness as making one trustworthy for service to God.

THE CHRISTIAN PRENUPTIAL AGREEMENT

Now the overseer is to be above reproach, faithful to his wife, temperate, self-controlled, respectable, hospitable, able to teach (1 Timothy 3:2).

A deacon must be faithful to his wife and must manage his children and his household well (1 Timothy 3:12).

An elder must be blameless, faithful to his wife, a man whose children believe and are not open to the charge of being wild and disobedient (Titus 1:6).

Give proper recognition to those widows who are really in need ... No widow may be put on the list of widows unless she is over sixty, has been faithful to her husband, and is well known for her good deeds, such as bringing up children, showing hospitality, washing the feet of the Lord's people, helping those in trouble and devoting herself to all kinds of good deeds (1 Timothy 5:3, 9-10).

5. Godly Roles

Other than our relationship with God, there is nothing more satisfying to the soul than deeply connecting with our spouse. It's a spiritual paradise. God created us with a need for this wonderful relationship, and for that reason, marriage is a gift. But we've also heard that "marriage is work." How can that be?

If you want something to last forever, you treat it differently. You shield it and protect it. You never abuse it. You don't expose it to the elements. You don't make it common or ordinary. If it ever becomes tarnished, you lovingly polish it until it gleams like new. It becomes special because you have made it so, and it grows more beautiful and precious as time goes by.
— F. Burton Howard

WHAT DOES GOD WANT FOR YOU?

Marriage is a gift with a responsibility ... to shield, protect, shelter, polish, and love your husband/wife unconditionally. These are the instructions that the Creator told us will help us to attain and maintain a long-lasting, deeply satisfying marriage relationship:

Job Description for Both:

> *Submit to one another out of reverence for Christ (Ephesians 5:21).*

> *Each man should have sexual relations with his own wife, and each woman with her own husband. The husband should fulfill his marital duty to his wife, and likewise the wife to her husband. The wife does not have authority over her own body but yields it to her husband. In the same way, the husband does not have authority over his own body but yields it to his wife. Do not deprive each other except perhaps by mutual consent and for a time, so that you may devote yourselves to prayer. Then come together again so that Satan will not tempt you because of your lack of self-control (1 Corinthians 7:2b-5).*

Job Descriptions for Husbands:

> *Husbands, love your wives, just as Christ loved the Church and gave himself up for her to make her holy, cleansing her by the washing with water through the word, and to present her to himself as a radiant Church, without stain or wrinkle or any other blemish, but holy and blameless. In this same way, husbands ought to love their wives as their own bodies. He who loves his wife loves himself (Ephesians 5:25-28).*

THE CHRISTIAN PRENUPTIAL AGREEMENT

Husbands, in the same way be considerate as you live with your wives, and treat them with respect as the weaker partner and as heirs with you of the gracious gift of life, so that nothing will hinder your prayers (1 Peter 3:7).

Enjoy life with your wife (Ecclesiastes 9:9a).

Husbands, love your wives and do not be harsh with them (Colossians 3:19).

If a man has recently married, he must not be sent to war or have any other duty laid on him. For one year he is to be free to stay at home and bring happiness to the wife he has married (Deuteronomy 24:5).[27]

Job Descriptions for Wives:

The wife must respect her husband (Ephesians 5:33b).

The husband is the head of the wife as Christ is the Head of the Church, His body, of which He is the Savior (Ephesians 5:23).

Wives, submit yourselves to your husbands, as is fitting in the Lord (Colossians 3:18).

Wives, in the same way submit yourselves to your own husbands so that, if any of them do not believe the word, they may be won over without words by the behavior of their wives (1 Peter 3:1).

WHAT DOES GOD WANT FOR YOU?

> *Teach the older women to be reverent in the way they live*
> *... Then they can urge the younger women to love their*
> *husbands and children, to be self-controlled and pure, to be*
> *busy at home, to be kind, and to be subject to their husbands,*
> *so that no one will malign the word of God (Titus 2:3-5).*

There are a number of scriptures that admonish women not to be quarrelsome. See Proverbs 19:13; 21:9, 19; 25:24; 27:15.

"Helper" and Submission

Our God-given roles display the beauty of maleness and femaleness, both of which are characteristics of God, as He made us in His image. God made women to be suitable "helpers." (See Genesis 2:18.) Unfortunately, some Christians have taken this to mean that women are to be servants of their husbands, especially in light of passages that say a wife is to submit. Some Christians have taught that husbands are to be authoritarian. There are two problems with these interpretations.

First, the Hebrew word for helper is "ezer," which is a word that God uses to describe Himself as our Helper. (See Exodus 18:4.) Unless you believe that God is our servant and we are to rule over Him, then to believe that the husband is to be an authoritarian master in the home is unfounded.

Secondly, the Bible says: *Now as the Church submits to Christ, so also wives should submit to their husbands in everything (Ephesians 5:24).* But the word "submit" used in this passage is not submission as ruler over servant, but rather one who desires the best for, or wants to help the spouses serve God's purposes.

This does not mean that husbands are not the ultimate authority in their home. The Bible states: *The husband is the head of the wife as Christ is the head of the Church, his body, of which he is the Savior (Ephesians 5:23).* In fact, being a husband means answering

89

THE CHRISTIAN PRENUPTIAL AGREEMENT

to God for not only his behavior, but also for his wife's. The buck stops with the man.

That being said, God calls husbands to lead as Jesus did for His Church. When Jesus walked this earth, He did not demand His rightful position, but instead taught that we are to be servants. The following passage takes place at the Last Supper. Jesus, knowing that His time to sacrifice His life was drawing near, took on the role of ultimate servanthood by washing the feet of His disciples.

> *When He had finished washing their feet, He put on His clothes and returned to His place. "Do you understand what I have done for you?" He asked them. "You call me 'Teacher' and 'Lord,' and rightly so, for that is what I am. Now that I, your Lord and Teacher, have washed your feet, you also should wash one another's feet. I have set you an example that you should do as I have done for you. Very truly I tell you, no servant is greater than his master, nor is a messenger greater than the one who sent him. Now that you know these things, you will be blessed if you do them" (John 13:12-17).*

This topic goes beyond the scope of this book, but it is important that you do not get trapped into bad thinking that can cause unnecessary damage to a new marriage. For a great and freeing clarification of gender roles, I recommend Dr. Larry Crabb's book, *Fully Alive: A Biblical Vision of Gender that Frees Men and Women to Live beyond Stereotypes.*

In his "Love and Respect" video conference course, Dr. Emerson Eggerichs states that, based on Ephesians 5:33, a man's deepest need is to be respected and a woman's greatest need is to be loved (emotionally). He goes on to suggest that because men respect naturally, God does not need to tell them to do that. Likewise, because women love naturally, they do not need to be reminded to love.[28] While both men and women need both love and respect to some extent, perhaps he has a point. However, both

WHAT DOES GOD WANT FOR YOU?

(emotional) love and respect are two forms of actively loving your spouse. Indeed, if you summarize all of the roles God gave us in marriage, do they not all boil down to one role and one job — to love your spouse sacrificially and unconditionally until death do you part?

6. Equally Yoked

Being unequally yoked is an agricultural concern related to plowing or pulling a wagon. A yoke is a device that goes over the head of animals that rests on their shoulders, allowing them to pull great weights. Putting two different animals in the dual-yoke may cause disastrous results. One may want to go and the other not, or one may bear the entire burden because it is stronger, exhausting the worker, and possibly rendering him useless.

The following passage of Scripture is commonly cited for this subject. While this passage is really a warning against becoming involved with idolatry (which was rampant in Corinth), the premise was that those who lived there were associating closely with idol worshippers. Unbelievers, by definition, are idol worshippers. They worship themselves and any number of worldly idols. Therefore, this passage of Scripture is still an applicable warning to the believing fiancé.

> *Do not be yoked together with unbelievers. For what do righteousness and wickedness have in common? Or what fellowship can light have with darkness? What harmony is there between Christ and Belial? Or what does a believer have in common with an unbeliever? What agreement is there between the temple of God and idols? For we are the temple of the living God. As God has said: "I will live with them and walk among them, and I will be their God, and they will be my people." Therefore, "Come out from them and be separate, says the Lord. Touch no unclean thing, and I will receive you." And, "I will be a Father to you, and you will be my sons and daughters, says the Lord Almighty" (2 Corinthians 6:14-18).*

THE CHRISTIAN PRENUPTIAL AGREEMENT

Unfortunately, many who marry unbelievers do so believing that they may be able to change them. Consider that Judas Iscariot lived with Jesus Messiah for three years, personally hearing His teaching and seeing His miracles; yet he was never saved. The more likely result is that their attempts to convert their spouses will push their spouses away, leaving them either very lonely in their marriages or divorced.

My cousin dated a man for many years. He would not marry her because she was not a Christian. Eventually she recognized God's love for her, and she accepted His gift of eternal life. They were married shortly after, and had a wonderfully God-honoring marriage.

On the other hand, most of the Christians who have ended up in my office after filing for divorce were unequally yoked, but had hoped to convert their spouses. For the Christians I have known who did not divorce, they live in one of the loneliest places on the planet.

If you are engaged to an unbeliever, how can the new "us" honor God with your marriage? As it relates to a prenuptial agreement, is it even possible to have an agreement that honors God if your fiancé is an unbeliever? Like my cousin's husband, you would be well advised to hold off until your fiancé becomes a believer so that you do not find yourself spiritually alone in your marriage.

7. Covenant Agreement

Much has been made of the importance of the marriage covenant and how a covenant differs from a contract. However, except for the biblical implications, when you look up *covenant* in a secular dictionary, it is defined as a contract or agreement. A contract is an agreement between two or more parties in which each party obliges itself to do something or give up something. It can be oral or written. If a contract is not performed as agreed, then

WHAT DOES GOD WANT FOR YOU?

the harmed party may sue to compel performance or otherwise be compensated for losses that result from the lack of performance.

Is there really a difference between a contract and a covenant, or is the difference between how God treats His promises and how sinful men treat theirs? For a clearer understanding, we will examine the biblical context.

The word "covenant" is found 286 times in the NIV Bible. Clearly covenants are a hot topic for God. Here are some examples of the covenants God made with us:

- God made one of His first covenants with Noah. He promised to never again send a flood to cut off all life and to destroy the earth. He gave us a rainbow as a sign of that covenant. (See Genesis 9:11-13.)

- God gave us the Abrahamic Covenant in which He promised Abraham the land, the seed, and the blessing. (See Genesis 12:1-3, Genesis 13:14-17, and Genesis 15:18.)

- God gave us Jesus, who said: *Then he took a cup, and when he had given thanks, he gave it to them, saying, "Drink from it, all of you. This is my blood of the covenant, which is poured out for many for the forgiveness of sins" (Matthew 26:27-28).*

- *For this reason Christ is the mediator of a new covenant, that those who are called may receive the promised eternal inheritance — now that he has died as a ransom to set them free from the sins committed under the first covenant (Hebrews 9:15).*

C.I. Scofield defined God's covenant in the following passage. Consider how the covenant that you are making with your fiancé measures up.

93

THE CHRISTIAN PRENUPTIAL AGREEMENT

A covenant is a sovereign pronouncement of God by which He establishes a relationship of responsibility (1) between Himself and an individual, (2) between Himself and mankind in general, (3) between Himself and a nation, or (4) between Himself and a specific human family. A covenant in one category may overlap others ... The covenants are normally unconditional in the sense that God obligates Himself in grace, by the unrestricted declaration, 'I will' to accomplish certain announced purposes, despite any failure on the part of the person or people with whom He covenants. The human response to the divinely announced purpose is always important, leading as it does to blessing for obedience and discipline for disobedience. But human failure is never permitted to abrogate the covenant or block its ultimate fulfillment.[29]

For marriage, God said this:

You ask, "Why?" It is because the LORD is the witness between you and the wife of your youth. You have been unfaithful to her, though she is your partner, the wife of your **marriage covenant** *(Malachi 2:14, emphasis added).*

Whether covenants, contracts, promises, vows, or oaths, God tells us:

It is better not to make a vow than to make one and not fulfill it. Do not let your mouth lead you into sin. And do not protest to the temple messenger, "My vow was a mistake." Why should God be angry at what you say and destroy the work of your hands? Much dreaming and many words are meaningless. Therefore fear God (Ecclesiastes 5:5-7).

94

WHAT DOES GOD WANT FOR YOU?

The action promised is not the focus, but rather our heart attitude and the solemnity with which we take our covenants. God wants our relationship with our spouses to look like our relationship with Him. He keeps His covenants with us, His Church. In fact, a central theme of the Bible is that God loves us so much that He keeps and honors His covenants with us despite how many times we are unfaithful to Him.

The following passage demonstrates the difference between the relationship that God creates with us through His covenant, and a common contractual relationship.

> *"I am the good shepherd. The good shepherd lays down his life for the sheep. The hired hand is not the shepherd and does not own the sheep. So when he sees the wolf coming, he abandons the sheep and runs away. Then the wolf attacks the flock and scatters it. The man runs away because he is a hired hand and cares nothing for the sheep.*
>
> *"I am the good shepherd; I know my sheep and my sheep know me — just as the Father knows me and I know the Father — and I lay down my life for the sheep" (John 10:11-15).*

The hired hand represents one who is under a contract without love. He is focused on himself. He promises to stay married as long as he is feeling fulfilled or loved. He doesn't agree to deal with rough times. His prenup ensures that he can escape marriage with minimal pain.

But the Good Shepherd loves His sheep and will lay down His life for them. He will stick it out even when He doesn't "feel" loved. In fact, the Bible says: *He was despised and rejected by mankind, a man of suffering, and familiar with pain. Like one from whom people hide their faces he was despised, and we held him in low esteem (Isaiah 53:3).* The Good Shepherd displays the love relationship Christians are called to enter with their spouses. Christian couples promise to stick it out when the going gets tough, even when they are despised and rejected.

THE CHRISTIAN PRENUPTIAL AGREEMENT

God made a number of covenants with us. He said that if we upheld His covenant law, then He would save us. We did not live up to our end of the bargain, because we did not uphold the law. The consequence for breaking the covenant is death. But God loves us so much that He not only continues to uphold His end of the deal, but He also paid the punitive damages for us so that we could escape eternal separation from Him. Are you ready to do that for your spouse when they don't hold up their "end of the deal"?

8. Godly Love

Love is patient, love is kind. It does not envy, it does not boast, it is not proud. It does not dishonor others, it is not self-seeking, it is not easily angered, it keeps no record of wrongs. Love does not delight in evil but rejoices with the truth. It always protects, always trusts, always hopes, always perseveres. Love never fails (1 Corinthians 13:4-8a).

Do not let any unwholesome talk come out of your mouths, but only what is helpful for building others up according to their needs, that it may benefit those who listen ... Get rid of all bitterness, rage and anger, brawling and slander, along with every form of malice. Be kind and compassionate to one another, forgiving each other, just as in Christ God forgave you (Ephesians 4:29, 31-32).

When citizens sign up for the military, they are agreeing to die for a cause. Secret service agents must be willing to take a bullet for the President. How deep is your love for your fiancé? Would you die for him/her?

You see, at just the right time, when we were still powerless, Christ died for the ungodly. Very rarely will anyone die for a righteous person, though for a good person someone

96

WHAT DOES GOD WANT FOR YOU?

might possibly dare to die. But God demonstrates his own love for us in this: While we were still sinners, Christ died for us. Since we have now been justified by his blood, how much more shall we be saved from God's wrath through him! For if, while we were God's enemies, we were reconciled to him through the death of his Son, how much more, having been reconciled, shall we be saved through his life! (Romans 5:6-10).

9. Children

Historically, little girls have grown up playing with baby dolls. God planted within women a desire to nurture and love babies. Perhaps this is why when women look at newborns, they see beautiful bundles of joy, while men just see odd-looking creatures. Of recent years, however, by the time young women are high school age, they are decreasingly interested in the ministry of motherhood. Is parenting a ministry? Does God want us to have and raise children?

Various passages in the Bible indicate that God desires for us to have children (many children, in fact), and that they are a reward and a blessing. In the Garden of Eden, after God had created man:

God blessed them and said to them, "Be fruitful and increase in number; fill the earth and subdue it. Rule over the fish in the sea and the birds in the sky and over every living creature that moves on the ground" (Genesis 1:28).

The name "Eve" means "life" or "the giver of life." Indeed, she brought the first baby into the world.

After the flood, God restarted mankind using Noah and his family. *Then God blessed Noah and his sons, saying to them, "Be fruitful and increase in number and fill the earth" (Genesis 9:1).*

Later, during the time when the Israelites returned to Jerusalem and were rebuilding the city, the book of Malachi questions: *Has*

97

THE CHRISTIAN PRENUPTIAL AGREEMENT

not the one God made you? You belong to him in body and spirit. And what does the one God seek? Godly offspring (Malachi 2:15).

From these passages it's clear that God's original purpose for women was to bear children and for marriages to produce godly offspring. The Bible goes on to tell us in a number of places that children are gifts from God. For example:

Children are a heritage from the LORD, offspring a reward from him. Like arrows in the hands of a warrior are children born in one's youth. Blessed is the man whose quiver is full of them (Psalm 127:3-5a).

When they see among them their children, the work of my hands, they will keep my name holy; they will acknowledge the holiness of the Holy One of Jacob, and will stand in awe of the God of Israel (Isaiah 29:23).

What does it mean when couples decide they don't want children or they want to limit the number that they have? Are your reasons God-honoring or self-centered? For example, some couples may decide against having children because of a family history of birth defects. Pregnancy may endanger certain women's lives. Perhaps you have been called into a ministry where you will be living in dangerous living conditions.

For those who cannot have children or for medical reasons decide not to, is there a reason why you would not provide foster care or even adopt?

Religion that God our Father accepts as pure and faultless is this: to look after orphans and widows in their distress (James 1:27a).

10. No Divorce

God provided man with rules for divorce. This was not because He desires for us to divorce, but He makes allowances for it, as outlined below.

For some of the New Testament passages to make sense, it's helpful to understand some of the cultural practices of the day. Some men were marrying women and when the women no longer pleased them, they would give them a certificate of divorce. Then they would marry another woman, and the pattern would continue. They sometimes decided to take a previous wife back. It was virtually a form of prostitution. This was not God's intention when He made the allowance, as can be seen in the following passages.

If a man marries a woman who becomes displeasing to him because he finds something indecent about her, and he writes her a certificate of divorce, gives it to her and sends her from his house, and if after she leaves his house she becomes the wife of another man, and her second husband dislikes her and writes her a certificate of divorce, gives it to her and sends her from his house, or if he dies, then her first husband, who divorced her, is not allowed to marry her again after she has been defiled. That would be detestable in the eyes of the LORD. Do not bring sin upon the land the LORD your God is giving you as an inheritance (Deuteronomy 24:1-4).

Another thing you do: You flood the LORD's altar with tears. You weep and wail because he no longer looks with favor on your offerings or accepts them with pleasure from your hands. You ask, "Why?" It is because the LORD is the witness between you and the wife of your youth. You have been unfaithful to her, though she is your partner, the wife of your marriage covenant.

THE CHRISTIAN PRENUPTIAL AGREEMENT

Has not the one God made you? You belong to him in body and spirit. And what does the one God seek? Godly offspring. So be on your guard, and do not be unfaithful to the wife of your youth.

"The man who hates and divorces his wife," says the LORD, *the God of Israel, "does violence to the one he should protect," says the* LORD *Almighty.*

So be on your guard, and do not be unfaithful (Malachi 2:13-16).

Jesus says: *"It has been said, 'Anyone who divorces his wife must give her a certificate of divorce.' But I tell you that anyone who divorces his wife, except for sexual immorality, makes her the victim of adultery, and anyone who marries a divorced woman commits adultery" (Matthew 5:31-32).*

"Haven't you read," [Jesus] replied, "that at the beginning the Creator 'made them male and female,' and said, 'For this reason a man will leave his father and mother and be united to his wife, and the two will become one flesh'? So they are no longer two, but one flesh. Therefore what God has joined together, let no one separate" (Matthew 19:4-6).

Jesus replied, "Moses permitted you to divorce your wives because your hearts were hard. But it was not this way from the beginning. I tell you that anyone who divorces his wife, except for sexual immorality, and marries another woman commits adultery" (Matthew 19:8-9).

To the married I give this command (not I, but the Lord): A wife must not separate from her husband. But if she does, she must remain unmarried or else be reconciled to her husband. And a husband must not divorce his wife.

WHAT DOES GOD WANT FOR YOU?

> *To the rest I say this (I, not the Lord): If any brother has a wife who is not a believer and she is willing to live with him, he must not divorce her. And if a woman has a husband who is not a believer and he is willing to live with her, she must not divorce him. For the unbelieving husband has been sanctified through his wife, and the unbelieving wife has been sanctified through her believing husband. Otherwise your children would be unclean, but as it is, they are holy.*
>
> *But if the unbeliever leaves, let it be so. The brother or the sister is not bound in such circumstances; God has called us to live in peace. How do you know, wife, whether you will save your husband? Or, how do you know, husband, whether you will save your wife? (1 Corinthians 7:10-16).*

There is no question that God hates divorce, but allows it because our "hearts were hard." Does this mean that God really doesn't want us to divorce at all — even if we have been betrayed? To answer this question, we have to start with God.

God tells us that marriage is a reflection of His relationship with us. Jesus is the Bridegroom and we (the Church) are His Bride. As His Bride we have turned away from God over and over, looking to and worshipping other idols in our lives. The book of Hosea describes how Israel prostituted herself, and yet Hosea continued to take her back at God's direction. That's how God fulfills His covenant ... unconditionally. God does not divorce us. He patiently waits for us to recognize our sin, repent, and return to Him.

Suppose Jack finds out that Jill has been cheating on him. She is unrepentant and has moved out to live with her lover. What does God want Jack to do? The kneejerk reaction is to file for divorce because Jack has "biblical grounds" for divorce. An alternative is for Jack to wait to see what God does in Jill's life. Jill may be convicted of her sin, repent, and ask Jack to take her back. If she is truly repentant, would it not be better for their marriage to be restored? Isn't God the God of restoration? Isn't that what He does for us every time we sin?

THE CHRISTIAN PRENUPTIAL AGREEMENT

Chances are Jill will file for divorce leaving Jack no choice, and Jack will find himself divorced. In that case, should Jack remarry? God says he's free to do so.

What about abuse, addiction, or imprisonment? If you are in physical danger, flee the situation and get immediate help. Beyond danger, these issues are not easy to deal with, but neither are they automatic reasons to divorce. Divorce should be the last resort, taking great care and much time to work through the situation and the issues. If you find yourself in one of these circumstances, be sure to seek wise counsel and professional help. Your ultimate goal should be to honor God and hopefully work toward your spouse's restoration to the Kingdom.

Finally, even if divorce becomes a reality, are you ever excused from loving your spouse? You are promising to love them until you die. They become your mission field and you declare that you want the best for them. I am not talking about becoming best friends. In fact, loving your ex-spouse may mean tough love and taking actions to avoid enabling them. But it certainly doesn't mean harboring resentment and hatred. It also means releasing your ex to God.

At this point, it is important to search your soul to be sure that you can promise to love your spouse as God intended so that you will not face divorce. Can you truly love them more than yourself? Do you want what's best for them? Will you help them to be the person God wants them to be?

Do nothing out of selfish ambition or vain conceit. Rather, in humility value others above yourselves, not looking to your own interests but each of you to the interests of the others (Philippians 2:3-4).

WHAT DOES GOD WANT FOR YOU?

Take some time to do Preparation Exercise 7: "Do You Really Mean 'For Better or Worse'?" Examine your heart as you read the examples. Then do the Preparation Exercise 8: "A Tale of Two Households." When you are done, share under what conditions you believe Christians should divorce and how you believe God calls Christians to behave when they divorce or are divorced. You will need to understand this as part of preparing your prenup. Recognize that it could be you who falls, so try to remember that you can only be responsible for your own life and choices. Just as God deals with you, your spouse is God's to deal with.

Lastly, make plans for how to avoid divorce. There is a section in Chapter 8 entitled, "Provisions to Inoculate Your Marriage from Divorce" that covers ways to build your marriage to avoid divorce.

Blessing

May God infuse your hearts with knowledge of His ways and may you seek to honor God by weaving His laws and precepts into your prenup, releasing His power into your marriage.

Part II

Practical Application

How to Get It Done

Whatever you do, work at it with all your heart, as working for the Lord, not for human masters, since you know that you will receive an inheritance from the Lord as a reward.
It is the Lord Christ you are serving
(Colossians 3:23-24).

THE CHRISTIAN PRENUPTIAL AGREEMENT

"Checking In ..."

Lifework Leadership employs a small group technique in which members "check in" and talk about how they are feeling and why. When they are done, they say, "Checking out." No one interrupts or comments on what the person is saying. This exercise helps you catch your breath from the busyness of life and gain perspective. Now is a good time for you to "check in" with your fiancé to be sure that you both are at the same point in this process — mentally and spiritually.

Checking in for perspective in this process, at this point, you should understand:

a) Why you need a prenup,

b) The power that a prenup unleashes into your marriage, and

c) How secular laws interface/conflict with God's laws.

Aside from this general knowledge, if you have done the exercises and answered the thought-provoking questions, you should now understand each other more profoundly. In fact, most couples at this point are at a minimum surprised, if not shocked, at how differently they view issues and want to handle various aspects of their lives together. This is a good thing. It's an opportunity to learn how to address differences together for "us" solutions.

Additionally, through this process you have been marking items in the book or keeping a list of what you want to include in your agreement. You have also been updating your idea of a marital homerun. Now you are ready to put it together.

Checking out ...

PRACTICAL APPLICATION: HOW TO GET IT DONE

Overview of the Process

Chapter 7   How To Put It All Together

Chapter 8   What To Include

Chapter 9   How To Get It Done

Chapter 10   Final Thoughts

THE CHRISTIAN PRENUPTIAL AGREEMENT

7

How To Put It All Together

1. Pray, Asking God for His Wisdom and Discernment.

Commit to the LORD whatever you do, and he will establish your plans (Proverbs 16:3).

2. Review Your Marital Homerun Goals.

During this process, you may have changed your ideas of what makes a marital homerun. Take time to review and update your plans to include new information, ideas, or attitudes that you have developed.

3. Understanding How Prenups Are Put Together

There are two parts of your prenuptial agreement that you will be helping construct: 1) the Recitals or Background section, and 2) the Provisions or Agreements section. I have included a sample prenuptial agreement in the Appendix so that you can get an idea of what one may look like. This is for demonstrative purposes only. It is not intended to be a template. It may not comply with legal standards, which is why you should consult an attorney.

The Recitals/Background section contains facts on which your agreements are based. They are usually presented as a list. If the section does not have a header, the facts may begin with the word "Whereas."

The Provisions/Agreements section contains what you are agreeing to do. For example, you may agree to raise your children in the Christian faith or to combine your assets upon marriage. These are sometimes enumerated without titles or may have "Therefore" before each agreement. They may also be under a section title such as "Agreements" or an opening paragraph that starts with "Now therefore."

These two parts act similarly to the "if/then" statements we learned in high school geometry classes, except that instead of the "ifs" being theories, you will have fact presented as recitals or background. It's more like "because" of the facts. The "then" statements are the agreements based upon the facts. For example, "*Because* we are getting married; *because* we desire to raise children; and *because* we are Christians, *then* we want to raise any children that we have, foster, or adopt in the Christian faith." However, the facts are generally not directly connected with the agreements. The recitals/background section is generally in one inclusive list followed by the agreements in another separate inclusive list.

HOW TO PUT IT ALL TOGETHER

4. Premarital Inventory

Most couples disagree on any number of issues. It is critical to the success of your marriage that you find out where you differ and how to resolve those differences.

Various organizations, premarital programs, books, and websites provide lists of questions that test your areas of agreement and disagreement on life's key issues. These may be related to work, faith, or family. I have provided such a list in the Preparation Exercise 9: "What Are You Going to Do About This?" It is critical that you and your fiancé answer questions and compare your answers in as many areas as possible.

There are also more sophisticated internet-based tools that use research to compare and measure compatibility. The provider of these tools may also have marriage coaches available to help you learn to communicate and guide you in critical areas of marriage, such as finance, work, children, etc. Two such programs are Prepare/Enrich®[30] and the Start Smart®.[31] I prefer the Start Smart® inventory report because it provides research for areas where you have differences of opinion with each other, as well as with research findings. Statistics show that couples who do a premarital program can reduce the risk of divorce by 30%.[32]

Once you determine your differences, learning how to work through them gives you great opportunities to define and create "us" in a positive way. Don't avoid issues hoping your fiancé will change. Don't yield on the "non-negotiables," such as foundational faith issues.

Working through differences does not necessarily mean compromise; but it does mean thinking outside your entrenched "me" ideas to find "us" solutions. You may not always agree, but the important thing is to learn is how to listen to your fiancé, understand, and appreciate their point of view. You are not marrying your twin. Hopefully, you are marrying someone who

THE CHRISTIAN PRENUPTIAL AGREEMENT

complements you. Your differences are often the very gifts that make you more useful for the Kingdom.

5. Preparation Exercises

 You should have completed all of the Preparation Exercises at this point. If not, go ahead and do them now.

6. Get Your Financial Disclosure Ready

Your attorneys will require you to share your financial information with each other. This is required by law in order for your prenup to be enforceable.

The financial disclosures usually list what you own (including their values), what you owe (including their balances) and what you earn. (You can find samples of financial disclosure online or get one from your attorney). Depending upon the complexity of your finances, some attorneys may even recommend preparing a package or book that includes copies of bank statements, investment statements, retirement accounts, ownership papers, appraisals of real or personal property, statements from creditors, paystubs, and tax returns.

Do not get married without sharing your financial information with each other. Too many couples marry without understanding their fiancé's financial situation, especially as it relates to debt. Even if your attorney does not require you to prepare a package with copies of your various financial documents, I recommend you sit down and show each other your actual documents so that you have full knowledge of the finances before you marry. Be sure to understand how much debt you will be starting your marriage with and how much that is going to impact your monthly cash flows going forward.

HOW TO PUT IT ALL TOGETHER

One area of disclosure that's often overlooked is previous marital settlement agreements or child support orders. If your fiancé has been married before or has parented a child, be sure to discuss the financial responsibilities that they carry as a result of those agreements, court orders, or any potential responsibilities that might arise in the future.

7. Check Your "Attitudimeter"

Airplanes have altimeters that measure the plane's altitude. For marriage, we need an "attitudimeter." The scale ranges from selfish on one end to self-sacrifice on the other.

One of the hardest things to do while working through this process is to stay focused on the "us" you are creating and not the "me" you are leaving behind. It's easy when dealing with property to drift back to the state of self-protection. Staying on the self-sacrifice end of the attitudimeter is the greatest challenge you will face in marriage.

Remember ...

Start with the end in mind. Be careful to avoid getting trapped in the mindset of the secular world that tends to focus on temporal things.

Therefore, with minds that are alert and fully sober, set your hope on the grace to be brought to you when Jesus Christ is revealed at his coming (1 Peter 1:13).

THE CHRISTIAN PRENUPTIAL AGREEMENT

What To Include

Hopefully, you have been compiling a list of provisions you would like to include in your agreement. Take those with you when you go to see your attorney. We will review some of the things you might wish to include in the balance of this chapter.

Attorneys who routinely prepare prenuptial agreements will include standard provisions that are required to make them legally enforceable, as well as those that they have previously included in secular prenups. However, your Christian prenup will differ significantly in its focus and purpose, thereby sometimes requiring different or additional language. Many of these differences were covered in the section, "What Does God Want for You?" Remember that the goal of your agreement is to provide covenant protection for your fiancé, not legal coverage for you.

You may wish to include some provisions that may not be legal in nature. For example, you may agree to have a ceremony to renew your vows annually on your anniversary. This may not be enforceable. However, just because a provision is not enforceable does not mean that you should not include it. Lawyers have crafty little clauses called "severability" clauses, which allow the rest of the document to stand even when one provision is not enforceable.

THE CHRISTIAN PRENUPTIAL AGREEMENT

If you have a lot of unenforceable clauses, an alternative might be to prepare a separate agreement or list of provisions to which you aspire. You might call this your "Play Book," "Marriage Roadmap," or "Guide to Marital Bliss." There are two reasons why you might want to separate out the unenforceable provisions:

1. Because your attorney says so.

2. Because the provisions contained in it are of a nature where they would be modifiable as you move through various stages of life. For example, you may want to put your children in Christian schools, but when they get to be school age, you agree that you want to homeschool.

Having an annually set date set to update your separate agreement is a nice way to gain perspective of your lives together and gives you an opportunity for a course correction. New Year's Day and anniversaries are nice, natural choices for this exercise. It may help you keep from "growing apart."

WHAT TO INCLUDE

1. Recognition of God, Faith, and Sin

How will you demonstrate your faith and belief in God and His laws and precepts in your agreement? Among the recitals at the beginning of your agreement, you may wish to include statements related to your faith, such as recognition that:

- God ordained marriage.

- God is the ultimate authority for your marriage.

- God intended us to become one flesh and to leave our parents and cleave to our spouse. (See Genesis 2:24.)

- Your faith is central to your marriage.

- God intended husbands and wives to fulfill the roles He gave us in marriage, and possibly even list what you believe those roles are.

- God called us to love one another as defined in 1 Corinthians 13:4-8a.

- God's called us to share our bodies sexually, which includes not withholding sex from one another. (See 1 Corinthians 7:3-5.)

- God calls us into a covenant relationship.

- God hates divorce, and He never ordains it, but allows it in certain circumstances such as adultery and desertion of an unbeliever.

- Man is utterly depraved. (See Romans 3:23.)

- Man needs forgiveness.

If you have prepared a statement of faith, you may wish to simply attach it and reference it.

THE CHRISTIAN PRENUPTIAL AGREEMENT

2. *Christian Vows*

Including your vows may be the most important statements in your prenup. Agree to love, honor, respect, trust, cherish, encourage, and support each other according to God's holy ordinances. Agree to forsake all others. Agree that you will stay together in good times and bad, for better or worse, for richer or poorer, in sickness and in health, in joy and in sorrow, in failure and in triumph, until death do you part. Acknowledge that these are actions that you will do regardless of how you are feeling or whether your spouse is reciprocating, as Christ died for His Bride even when we were not reciprocating. (See Romans 5:8.)

WHAT TO INCLUDE

3. Provisions Related to Parents

We have a tricky balancing act trying to honor our parents while leaving them and cleaving to our spouses. It will honor your parents to acknowledge their contributions to your lives. But when it comes to your new lives together, you will most likely feel pulled to continue patterns with your parents that may be injurious to your marriage. (See Preparation Exercise: "Keeping In-Laws from Becoming Out-Laws.")

Be sure to address your commitment to forsake all others, including your parents, when it comes to accepting advice, creating your own traditions, and making decisions for "us."

THE CHRISTIAN PRENUPTIAL AGREEMENT

4. Provisions for Godly Roles

We reviewed biblical roles for men and women in Chapter 6, "What Does God Want for You?" What roles will you assume? Do you have plan for decision-making? Who will be the financial provider? Who will be responsible for paying the bills? Who will be responsible for preparing the tax returns? Who will be responsible for oil changes?

Be careful with the attitudes that may result from making these types of agreements. Just because the tasks are in your spouse's column does not mean that you shouldn't do them. Furthermore, it is important that you do not allow these lists to become a source of resentment when someone isn't living up to "their end of the deal." Jesus, who was entitled to be worshipped as King, came as a Servant, even washing the feet of His disciples. Your roles should be guidelines to help you stay focused on what honors God, not yourself. It should be your honor that you have the opportunity love and serve your spouse.

WHAT TO INCLUDE

5. Provisions for Finances

In consideration of the negative impact that financial stress can have on marital success, having agreements on how you will handle money may help you avoid years of financial misery, and may even save your marriage. Consider the following:

- Who is going to work and for what periods

- Expected age of retirement

- Amount of tithe and other church giving

- Amount of charitable giving to other organizations

- How you will avoid debt and pay off any that you have

- If you will hold off on children until debt is repaid

- How much you want to spend on housing and whether you want to buy or rent

- Amount you are willing to spend on education, whether it is for you or for your children to attend Christian/private schools, vocational schools, or college

- Whether you will invest in a 529 college savings plan or other college prepaid fund for your children

- Retirement savings goal

- Use of credit for purchasing cars versus saving up for car replacement

121

THE CHRISTIAN PRENUPTIAL AGREEMENT

- Use of credit cards, such as no more charges than can be paid in a month

- Use of routine budget or business meetings to discuss and plan your finances

- Titling of bank accounts

- Use of financial advisors

- Use of savings accounts for replacement of items such as roofs, appliances, etc.

- Food budget for groceries, work lunches, coffee house coffee, eating out, etc.

- Clothing and personal care budget

- Vacation/recreation budgeting

- Who will handle the day-to-day recording of the finances

- Method of recording finances and record retention (paper/electronic)

- Who will prepare taxes (you or professional)

WHAT TO INCLUDE

6. Provisions for Children

Provisions for children are tricky, because God may have different plans for children than you do. You may ultimately find that you are unable to conceive or you may have an unplanned child. You may have a special needs child. Understanding that God is in control and that all children are really His will help you relax and honor God in this area. Flexibility is key to marital success.

That being said, there are certain provisions that you should include in your prenuptial agreement that may be critical legally. Be sure to include in your legal document that you want them to be raised as Christians. If you do not state this in a legal document, and your spouse later decides they are an atheist or pursue another religion, your children may be exposed to false doctrine, and there may be nothing that you can do about it. (I have witnessed this too many times.)

Some attorneys question whether this is enforceable. One family-law judge I spoke to said it is, but that does not mean that another would not disagree. Regardless, by including this provision, at least you have done all you can to protect your children and honor God.

Beyond faith issues, are parenting styles. This may be one of the greatest sources of conflict in marriage, because couples often have different views of how children should be raised. Our beliefs about how children should be raised are usually based upon how we were raised. The most common conflicts occur when one parent is an enforcer and the other is lenient or detached. Find out what your spouse believes about rearing children and decide how you want to parent. Remember to stay flexible but focused on what honors God. I guarantee that your ideas about raising children will change once you have them. We all believe we will do a better job than all those other parents who have unruly children.

123

THE CHRISTIAN PRENUPTIAL AGREEMENT

 (There are great discussion builders on this topic in the Preparation Exercise: "What Are You Going to Do About This?")

In the event of divorce, calculation of child support payments are usually an operation of law, and therefore, various aspects of your agreement related to supporting children may be overridden. For example, in Florida, there are formulas for determining the amount of child support based on what the parents earn (or could earn). Therefore, unless you are agreeing to an amount that exceeds the minimum required by law, the formulas will apply. You can even just agree to the state formulas.

If you have agreed for the mother to stay home to raise the children and not work, state that in your agreement. Otherwise, the judge may "impute" income to the mother based on her ability to work, which would reduce the child support payments, and may force her back into the workforce. Your attorney can direct you in this area.

Whatever you decide in this area, remember that God is ultimately in control and hold on to your agreements loosely. This is one of those areas where the saying often becomes a reality: "Man plans. God laughs." He has a greater purpose for your life then you can ever imagine.

> *"For I know the plans I have for you,"* declares the LORD, *"plans to prosper you and not to harm you, plans to give you hope and a future" (Jeremiah 29:11).*

WHAT TO INCLUDE

Children of this relationship created before marriage

If you already have children borne of this relationship or are pregnant with a child of this relationship, then you have some special issues to deal with. Being pregnant may possibly be a factor that might cause your prenup to be questioned for its validity. There may also be issues of feeling trapped, which can lead to resentment. Get counseling, even if you feel like you don't need it, just to be sure that you have dealt with any uncovered attitudes.

Consider the following for your agreement:

- If you are pregnant when you marry, disclose the pregnancy in the agreement. (Your attorney will most likely require this.)

- Decide when and how you will disclose to your child(ren) that you were not married when they were conceived or born. (Eventually they will figure out the math.)

- If the child(ren) was/were born prior to marriage, and they bear their mother's maiden name, determine if you want to change their names.

- If the father is not listed on the birth certificate, determine if you will take measures to add him to the certificate.

- Ratify the agreement post-marriage to indicate that you were not coerced into signing the agreement.

THE CHRISTIAN PRENUPTIAL AGREEMENT

Children of previous relationships

Step-parenting is difficult, but not impossible to overcome. In her book, *For Better or Worse*, Dr. Hetherington gives the following statistics: "simple stepfamilies" (where only one partner brought a child or children to the new marriage) divorced at a rate of 65%; when both partners had children from previous relationships ("complex stepfamilies") the divorce rate was slightly more than 70%.'[33] Your ability to handle blended families will be greatly affected by their ages when you marry, their ages when their birth parents broke up, and the involvement of the other parent in the children's lives.

Ron Deal is a well-known expert who helps couples enter second marriages with open eyes. His website is www.smartstepfamilies.com. Be sure to address the potential issues together and with a counselor before you marry. In your agreement, you may wish to incorporate mechanisms for honoring step-parents.

Inability to conceive

You may want to have children but find yourselves unable to conceive. In your agreement, if you find that you cannot conceive, you may wish to agree on:

- Foster parenting
- Adoption
- Using a surrogate mother or donated sperm
- Volunteering in children's activities or ministries as an alternative to parenting

WHAT TO INCLUDE

<u>No desire to have children.</u>

Some couples have decided not to have children. If you choose not to have children, then it is important to make provisions for birth control and for unplanned pregnancies.

It is not uncommon for both men and women to change their minds on this subject. Therefore, if you wish to state that it is not your intention at the outset to have children, you can also state what your plans will be if one of you changes his/her mind later or if there is an unplanned pregnancy. As with all agreements made which are not related to fundamental faith issues, remaining flexible for God's leading and honoring your spouse should be a priority in your marriage.

THE CHRISTIAN PRENUPTIAL AGREEMENT

7. Provisions for Homestead

In your agreement, you may wish to agree on:

- Where are you would like to live

- Openness to moving for job purposes

- Staying near elderly parents

- For military personnel, living in military housing

- Buying versus renting

WHAT TO INCLUDE

8. Provisions for Holidays, Vacations, and Recreation

How you will spend your holidays and vacations can become a sore point, especially if there are family traditions from your parents that you or they want you to continue to observe after you get married. Where will you go for Thanksgiving and Christmas or will you stay home?

Additionally, differences in ideas of how to spend your vacation/recreation time can be a sore point. Perhaps one of you is a camper and the other likes cruising. Deciding to alternate vacations may be a great alternative. It is important that each of you spend time doing activities that the other enjoys, even if it is not your cup of tea. This will build an incredible intimacy in your marriage.

In your agreement, you may wish to agree on:

- Where you plan to spend your holidays (home, parents, vacationing)

- How you like to use your vacation time (cruise, camp, RV, exotic, rustic, spending)

THE CHRISTIAN PRENUPTIAL AGREEMENT

9. Provisions for Medical Issues

Medical History

Do you know your fiancé's medical history? Would you be able to answer simple medical questions about them in an emergency? As I alluded to in the Introduction, my husband had a stroke a few months after our wedding. I found myself in the emergency room unable to answer the following questions:

Does he have allergies?

Does he have high blood pressure?

Any history of strokes in the family?

Any history of heart disease in the family?

What medications is he taking?

What kind of wife was I?

Could *you* answer these questions? Could you fill out a patient information form in an emergency room? Medical issues should be addressed and plans made for them.

While this information most likely does not belong in your prenup, exchanging medical data may save your lives. I recommend you start a medical journal or file before you marry to document the following:

- Names and phone numbers for doctors, including dentists and eye doctors

- Medical issues, such as allergies or diabetes

- Blood type

WHAT TO INCLUDE

- Medications

- Vaccinations

- History of surgeries and broken bones

- Sexual history, including abortion and sexually transmitted diseases

- Family medical history, including diseases such as cancer or heart disease

Medical Skeletons

Sometimes when we marry, we don't give full medical disclosure. There should be no secrets. If you have been previously sexually active, then you may put your spouse at risk for acquiring sexually transmitted diseases. If you have previously had an abortion, you are more at risk for breast cancer[34] and you may have difficulties with childbearing. The Mayo Clinic research shows abortion can be linked to:

- Vaginal bleeding during early pregnancy

- Preterm birth

- Low birth weight

- Placenta previa — when the placenta partially or completely covers the cervix, which can cause severe bleeding before or during delivery[35]

Are there medical skeletons in your closet? Have you disclosed your disabilities and sexual history to your fiancé? Unless your medical issues preclude you from bearing children or "normal sexual function," it is unlikely that your attorney will recommend

THE CHRISTIAN PRENUPTIAL AGREEMENT

including this information in your prenup. However, if some undisclosed medical issue of which you were fully aware later emerges that shows a deceitful intent (like knowing that you cannot bear children, but covering up this fact), it may be grounds for the annulment of your marriage.

Medical Surrogate

Who do you want making medical decisions for you in the event you are disabled and cannot make them for yourself? What does your state dictate for medical surrogacy? If you don't like the default mode for your state, you may wish to specifically name your medical surrogate in your prenup.

WHAT TO INCLUDE

10. Provisions to Inoculate Your Marriage from Divorce

Secular divorce planning generally involves who gets what. The most significant divorce planning that you can do is to agree on how to build "us" and, in the process, avoid divorce. A proactive plan is the best defense against divorce and behaviors that can lead there. These are some things you might include in your prenup:

- Have a daily prayer time together.

- Have a regular date night so that you stay connected.

- Attend marriage conferences at least yearly.

- Have a romantic getaway annually.

- Review your prenuptial agreements on your anniversary or as part of your New Year's activities.

- Renew your vows periodically.

- Stay engaged with marriage mentors.

- Seek counseling when one of you feels like your marriage is out of balance.

- Look only to each other for emotional, spiritual, and financial support — not parents, coworkers, or the opposite sex.

- Avoid spending time with the opposite sex, such as business lunches.

THE CHRISTIAN PRENUPTIAL AGREEMENT

- Avoid confiding personal information with or seeking emotional support from the opposite sex.

- Avoid pornography.

- Join accountability groups if an addictive behavior surfaces.

- Join together sexually at least weekly.

- Work through even the most extreme issues, possibly even agreeing not to file for divorce for some period of years to give God a chance to work out the issues.

- Avoid bringing up divorce in the heat of an argument.

- Declare not to separate except in certain conditions (like military service, periods of relocation, or physically abusive situations).

As with fire drills, having plans in place to escape the fire may be the very element that saves your marriage. It is also important to recognize the devastating effects of divorce on children before heading down that road. (See "What Is Divorce and Family Fragmentation Costing You?" in the Appendix.)

WHAT TO INCLUDE

11. Provisions for Divorce Alternatives

"Blessed are the peacemakers, for they will be called children of God" (Matthew 5:9).

First, and foremost, **violation of the terms of your prenup should not under any circumstances be the basis for filing for divorce.** Your prenup is a plan for a God-honoring marriage. Our Christianity means that we are to be filled with grace with each other, as God doles out grace to us.

* * * * *

Marriage was designed by God to be the union of two forgivers who have experienced the forgiveness of Jesus Christ.

* * * * *

Just as we struggle with the necessity of having a legal document for a sacred marriage, we also struggle with how to proceed when one spouse commits an act that is an allowance for divorce, such as adultery or abandonment. Do we just file for divorce and let the law take its course? First, let us examine what God says in these cases.

"If your brother or sister sins, go and point out their fault, just between the two of you. If they listen to you, you have won them over. But if they will not listen, take one or two others along, so that 'every matter may be established by the testimony of two or three witnesses.' If they still refuse to listen, tell it to the church; and if they refuse to listen even to the church, treat them as you would a pagan or a tax collector" (Matthew 18:15-17).

THE CHRISTIAN PRENUPTIAL AGREEMENT

First Corinthians 7:10-16 discusses divorcing unbelievers. This passage points out that our staying in the marriage may bring an unbeliever to belief. Perhaps the question to be asked in this situation should be: Is my happiness more important than the salvation of my spouse?

We honor God when we reconcile ourselves to each other and make peace. Therefore, our first actions should be attempting reconciliation if that is all possible. That would mean reconciling ourselves to God and to each other. During times of high conflict, this may seem impossible, but time and wise counsel will often open our eyes to paths to reconciliation. In order to honor God and give your spouse the greatest opportunity to be reconciled to God, it is imperative that we exhaust all options before throwing in the towel.

Giving yourself time before taking action will also give you time to see your own responsibility for the trouble in your marriage so that you can fix yourself. People getting divorces are always ready to point out the fault in the other, but rarely ready to accept their contribution to the problems. The movie, *Fireproof,* did a great job of showing how we must work on changing our own behavior during times of marital conflict.

Therefore, in your agreement it is important to construct the path to reconciliation. Some possible provisions for times of high conflict would be:

- Seek counseling together with a local counselor.

- Submit to a ruling body if your church provides such service.

- Attend a marriage intensive or marriage-in-crisis weekend with an organization that supplies such services.

- Allow a minimum time frame before filing for divorce.

- Allow a minimum separation period before filing for divorce.

WHAT TO INCLUDE

Time gives you perspective and a chance to consider all the ramifications of a possible divorce. Only Satan wins in divorce. Divorce has a rippling effect throughout your family that cannot be undone. Media makes divorce seem palatable, even expected. Divorce is a tearing of the flesh for which there can be some healing, but it always leaves a scar.

THE CHRISTIAN PRENUPTIAL AGREEMENT

12. Provision if Divorce Is Unavoidable

If you have exhausted all your reconciliation attempts or your spouse files for divorce unilaterally, then divorce may seem inevitable. It is important to understand that filing for divorce is technically filing a civil lawsuit against your spouse. The Bible has some very clear admonitions regarding lawsuits:

> *If any of you has a dispute with another, do you dare to take it before the ungodly for judgment instead of before the Lord's people? Or do you not know that the Lord's people will judge the world? And if you are to judge the world, are you not competent to judge trivial cases? Do you not know that we will judge angels? How much more the things of this life! Therefore, if you have disputes about such matters, do you ask for a ruling from those whose way of life is scorned in the church? I say this to shame you. Is it possible that there is nobody among you wise enough to judge a dispute between believers? But instead, one brother takes another to court — and this in front of unbelievers!*
>
> *The very fact that you have lawsuits among you means you have been completely defeated already. Why not rather be wronged? Why not rather be cheated? Instead, you yourselves cheat and do wrong, and you do this to your brothers and sisters. Or do you not know that wrongdoers will not inherit the kingdom of God? (1 Corinthians 6:1-9).*

In biblical times, husbands could give their wives certificates of divorce and quietly divorce them. Court appearances were not required. However, modern divorces, even if worked out between the parties without assistance, require filing a lawsuit and appearing before a judge to have their agreement ratified by the court and their marriage dissolved. There does not appear to be a way to avoid this. However, you can avoid having an ungodly

WHAT TO INCLUDE

judge hear and rule on the particulars of your divorce, such as property division or support.

Depending upon what your state allows, you may wish to do your own divorce or pursue a collaborative divorce, where you each hire attorneys and work together toward a resolution. By hiring Christian attorneys, you avoid bringing your dispute before unbelievers. You also avoid escalating litigation expenses that can arise in disputed matters.

If you cannot resolve your disputes amongst yourselves, then you may wish to hire Christian litigation attorneys and proceed to mediation, where you will have another opportunity to work through your issues.

If this does not succeed, is there a possible remedy in your state where you could hire a Christian arbitrator or a personal judge who could make a ruling on your divorce in light of Scripture and in light of secular law?

Perhaps the hardest thing to accept if you cannot come to an agreement is what Scripture says about not bringing your matters before ungodly judges. You are challenged with the following two questions: *Why not rather be wronged? Why not rather be cheated? (1 Corinthians 6:8)*. Ouch! This is one of those times when you have to search your soul to determine if you are willing to lay it all down to follow the Lord and trust Him for His provision.

Whatever you decide, after consulting with your attorney on what the law allows related to divorce, include in your prenup how you will proceed in the event of divorce. I suggest that you agree to:

- Provisions for divorce in your prenup in an attempt to avoid litigation over property division and support

- Promise to affirm the other parent to your children and do everything in your power to honor each other as father or mother.

139

THE CHRISTIAN PRENUPTIAL AGREEMENT

- Decide where you believe it would be best for the children to live and what schedule would be best for the children's emotional health.

- Use collaborative law as an alternative to full blown litigation.

- Use only Christian attorneys so as not to violate the instructions of 1 Corinthians 6:1-8.

- Agree to seek alternatives to having an ungodly judge rule on your divorce (to the extent that they exist), such as a Christian arbitrator or a private judge.

- Agree that you will not seek a secular court to resolve your dispute.

This is not an all-inclusive list. There may be other provisions that your attorney may suggest. But as with each element of what I have provided and with what your attorney recommends, pray and seek God's wisdom through His Word and through godly counsel.

9

How To Get It Done

You have now completed all of the work necessary to know what you want in your prenup. Now it's time to hire an attorney and get your prenup prepared.

It's going to cost. But compared to the other wedding expenses, it's a bargain. How much it costs depends upon factors like the complexity of the agreement and how prepared you are when you go to the attorney's office. According to TheKnot.com and the Wedding Channel, the average wedding in 2012 cost $28,427.[36] Breaking that down, the average cost of the reception venue is $12,905. Unless you are Donald Trump, it is unlikely your prenup will cost that much. Flowers are almost $2,000. They dry up and are gone within weeks of the wedding. Event planners are just over $1,800. If you were choosing between spending $1,800 on someone who helps you plan your marriage versus someone who helps you plan one day, which is the better dollar spent? How much more important is it to get the foundation in place for a marriage that will last a lifetime?

THE CHRISTIAN PRENUPTIAL AGREEMENT

1. Hiring Attorneys

Because there are two parties to a contract, each party should be represented by their own attorney. Usually one attorney drafts the agreement with their client, and then presents it to the other. The receiving party then reviews it and consults with his/her attorney. Not having two separate attorneys may cause the prenup to be questioned for enforceability.

When hiring, get recommendations for attorneys who prepare Christian prenups. Interview the attorneys first over the phone and then in person to be sure that they understand what you are trying to accomplish. Because this book contains a radically new premise, you may wish to provide them with a copy. Also, check the website www.ChristianPrenup.com.

Ask the prospective attorneys what they charge up front. Is it a fixed fee or is it hourly? You may wish to agree to a cap of a certain amount to be sure there are no cost overruns. Because the complexity of your agreement and the number of tweaks that may be required are unknown upfront, attorneys often shy away from flat fees.

Ask the attorney what documents and information they need from you to draft the agreement so that you can bring them along.

HOW TO GET IT DONE

2. Preparing to Meet with Your Attorney

First, ask God to prepare your heart and mind, because Satan will be working to keep it from getting done and trying to cause turmoil around the process. He will be working to get you focused on yourself, instead of the one with whom God is entrusting you.

Rejoice in the Lord always. I will say it again: Rejoice! Let your gentleness be evident to all. The Lord is near. Do not be anxious about anything, but in every situation, by prayer and petition, with thanksgiving, present your requests to God. And the peace of God, which transcends all understanding, will guard your hearts and your minds in Christ Jesus.

Finally, brothers and sisters, whatever is true, whatever is noble, whatever is right, whatever is pure, whatever is lovely, whatever is admirable — if anything is excellent or praiseworthy — think about such things. Whatever you have learned or received or heard from me, or seen in me — put it into practice. And the God of peace will be with you (Philippians 4:4-9).

Secondly, be organized. The quicker you can explain what you want to the attorney, the lower the fees. Put together a list of the provisions that are important to you. You may even provide them with a proforma prenup that you drafted together that you can just hand to the attorney. This may provide two benefits. First it will save time. It will also help reduce some of the "negotiations" because you have already agreed to provisions.

Along with the provisions you want, provide your attorney with the documents that they requested in an organized manner (in the specific order that they requested them). Already have these documents copied so that your attorney doesn't have to take time doing that.

Bringing this book may be helpful for you in case you need to reference anything.

143

THE CHRISTIAN PRENUPTIAL AGREEMENT

3. Meeting with Your Attorney (Drafter)

Open in prayer. Ask for God's guidance and direction over this process.

If you are the drafter of the agreement, explain what you are seeking from your prenup. The attorney will then explain the prenup process to you and will offer you a retainer agreement for you to read and sign. Read this carefully. Don't be afraid to ask questions and be sure that the attorney understands your goals. Sign after you have done the next couple of steps to be sure that your attorney can accurately gauge what they expect the fees and the process to be.

Provide your attorney with your list of provisions that you would like to include. Offer the book to them if you feel like they need clarification on your goals.

If you are planning to have an estate attorney later, you will likely have to hire a different attorney for this, as the attorney who handles your prenup may have a conflict of interest in doing your joint work after the marriage. Ask your attorney about this. Also ask your attorney what estate planning you can effectuate through the prenup.

Provide your attorney with your financial information. Be sure to go through it with them while you are there so that you can answer any questions and be sure that they understand and have everything they need.

After clarifying what you want and reviewing your financial situation, discuss how much it should cost to get it done. Now is the optimal time to sign the retainer agreement if you believe that the attorney fully comprehends your goals and you are comfortable with the expected costs.

The attorney will then draft an agreement (with or without your presence — this will depend upon their style of working). It may be more effective for you to be there while they draft it.

When they are done, review the draft, approve it, and then either they will send it to your fiancé, or you or your fiancé's attorney will take it.

HOW TO GET IT DONE

4. Reviewing the Draft

If your fiancé has prepared the draft with his/her attorney, then you will review the draft with your attorney.

First, you will have hired your attorney in a manner similar to that described above with opening in prayer, discussing your goals, and reviewing/signing a retainer agreement. Your fees should be less because your attorney is not drafting.

You may make some revisions that may then cause a bit of back and forth to tweak the agreement, but ultimately, there will be an agreement that is ready to sign.

THE CHRISTIAN PRENUPTIAL AGREEMENT

5. *Check It Twice*

When you have completed your prenup, take a moment to prayerfully consider if you have accomplished what you set out to do. Does your prenup:

- Honor God?

- Create and define your new "us"?

- Have a view to Heaven?

- Reflect Jesus' love as defined in 1 Corinthians 13?

- Reflect the vows and promises that you will make at the altar?

- Contain a clear declaration of your faith?

- Reflect God's plan, laws, and precepts for marriage?

- Reflect your homerun?

HOW TO GET IT DONE

6. Signing

When you are comfortable with the terms and that it is accomplishing your purposes and that it honors God, then it will be time to sign it.

Depending upon your state, it may need witnesses' and/or notary's signatures. The attorneys will direct when and where it is to be signed, whether jointly or at their individual offices.

If you would prefer to make it a ceremonial signing, discuss this with your attorneys. For example, you may wish to sign it just before your wedding ceremony. However, this may be problematic for enforceability reasons. Therefore, check with your attorneys if you are interested in a special signing ceremony.

THE CHRISTIAN PRENUPTIAL AGREEMENT

10

Final Thoughts

Now that you have completed your prenup, what will you do with it? Where will you keep it? How often will you review it? How will you use it?

1. Not a Weapon

Your prenup should never be used as a weapon during an argument, either physically by throwing it at one another or verbally by reminding the other of what is in it in a negative way. In fact, your prenup should be referenced as a source of joy and as a remembrance or celebration of your covenant. Using it during an argument would be akin to throwing a Bible at an unbeliever to try to make them accept the faith.

THE CHRISTIAN PRENUPTIAL AGREEMENT

2. Not an Excuse for Divorce

Life will throw you many curveballs during your marriage. Flexibility is the key to marital success. One of the dangers of having a prenup is that some couples may use it as an excuse for divorce.

For example, Theresa and Tommy agreed in their prenup that they were not going to have children. A decade passed. Couple by couple, their friends began to have children and become increasingly busy with their family lives. As Theresa approached her 35th birthday, she began to long for children of her own. When she brought this up to Tommy, instead of agreeing with her desires or sacrificing for her, he decided to enforce their prenup and divorce her.

Was Theresa justified in changing her mind? Was Tommy justified in filing for divorce? Can you see how when we begin to seek "justice" or our rights, our mindset turns to self-preservation instead of self-sacrifice? The agreements that you make in your prenup should *never* be your grounds for divorce. Your agreements should be a guide and a testimony to how you have honored God in all things, even when things don't go according to plan.

3. Subject to Modification

Your prenup may be modified any time you both agree. For example, you may have included plans to educate your children in Christian schools. However, when they get to school age, you decide that because you are in a good school district, you don't need to spend the money, so you modify your prenup. You may be able to do this modification in an addendum to your original prenup. Ask your attorney.

Because things change, you may wish to review your prenup on a regular basis, such as on your anniversary or on New Year's Day, to reflect changes in your goals and your married life.

FINAL THOUGHTS

4. Happily Ever After?

We started this journey by asking you to define what would be a homerun for your marriage. What will you have accomplished through your marriage after fifty years? What will your lives have counted for?

In his book, *Sacred Marriage*, Gary Thomas asks the question "What if God designed marriage to make us holy more than to make us happy?" The premise of his book is that God uses marriage to teach us truths about Himself, how to love and respect others, pray, expose our sin, teach forgiveness, and develop our spiritual calling.[37] I liken it to spiritual boot camp, where the more we are challenged, the more useful we become. Some of these lessons may not make us happy at the time, but they will bring us step by step closer to sanctification and holiness. In the end, that will produce unspeakable joy and a marriage that counts for eternity.

What does it take to accomplish this? While this passage was not intended as instructions for marriage, it gives us guidance as to a life lived that is worthy of our Lord. It reflects what we are called to do in marriage — imitate Christ's humility.

Therefore if you have any encouragement from being united with Christ, if any comfort from his love, if any common sharing in the Spirit, if any tenderness and compassion, then make my joy complete by being like-minded, having the same love, being one in spirit and of one mind. Do nothing out of selfish ambition or vain conceit. Rather, in humility value [your spouse] above yourselves, not looking to your own interests but each of you to the interests of the others.

In your relationships with one another, have the same mindset as Christ Jesus: Who, being in very nature God, did not consider equality with God something to be used to his own advantage; rather, he made himself nothing by taking the very nature of a servant, being made in human likeness. And

151

THE CHRISTIAN PRENUPTIAL AGREEMENT

being found in appearance as a man, he humbled himself by becoming obedient to death — even death on a cross! (Philippians 2:1-8).

This is the secret to accomplishing your goals, having a life worth living, and one that glorifies God.

Prayer for Your Marriage

May you achieve the homerun that you set out to accomplish for your marriage.
May you find deep love and companionship for your souls.
May you value your spouse above yourself.
May you be co-laborers and fellow sojourners who will stand together through it all.
May you relish every wonder-filled moment of life.
May you be vigilant for the attacks of the enemy and avoid giving him a foothold.
May you honor God with your marriage.
May you always remember that love is an action, and until death, do your part.
To God be the glory, forever. Amen.

Part III

Preparation Exercises

Building Material

*So whether you eat or drink or whatever you do,
do it all for the glory of God (1 Corinthians 10:31).*

Overview of the Exercises

1. Writing Your Marriage Vows

2. What Will Your Lives Count For?

3. Rules of Engagement

4. Writing Your Statement of Faith

5. Financial Planning

6. Keeping In-Laws from Becoming Out-Laws

7. Do You Really Mean "For Better or Worse"?

8. A Tale of Two Households

9. What Are You Going To Do about This?

PREPARATION EXERCISES

THE CHRISTIAN PRENUPTIAL AGREEMENT

Exercise 1

Writing Your Marriage Vows

What vows will you take during your wedding ceremony? Will you use "traditional" vows that your pastor or denomination suggests or will you write your own?

Check out various vows on the internet. It is interesting to see what vows various denominations use and some very creative vows that people have written.

These are some of the traditional words commonly used in ceremonies:

I, _____, take you, _____, to be my lawfully wedded wife/husband, to live together in the Holy Estate of Matrimony: to love, honor, respect, trust, cherish, encourage, and support you according to God's Holy ordinance, forsaking all others and keeping myself only unto you, for better or worse, for richer or poorer, in sickness and in health, in good times and in bad, in joy and in sorrow, in failure and in triumph, from this day forward until death do us part.

Study these words. They are the essence of what Christians are called to promise. I suggest incorporating these words in your prenuptial agreement.

Pray about the words you choose and be sure that you are truly committed to them.

158

PREPARATION EXERCISES

Our Vows...

THE CHRISTIAN PRENUPTIAL AGREEMENT

Exercise 2

What Will Your Lives Count For?

Sorry to be morbid, but perhaps the best way to measure the value of a life worth living is the view we get at a funeral. If everything goes the way you hope, what will people say about you at your funeral? Will your actions be a testimony to a life that honored God?

* * * * *

Only one life, 'twill soon be past, only what's done for Christ will last. —C. T. Studd

* * * * *

Take some time to write out a eulogy that you hope could be read at your funeral. Ask your fiancé to do the same. Exchange them and pray about how you can get there. Use these as your guide to formulating your marital homerun and writing your prenuptial.

PREPARATION EXERCISES

What will our lives count for?

THE CHRISTIAN PRENUPTIAL AGREEMENT

Exercise 3

Rules of Engagement

In times of conflict, nations commonly operate within their accepted "Rules of Engagement." This is a term that is used when an organization is planning to use force against someone or some group. They are meant to keep people within the bounds of some socially acceptable conduct. Rules of engagement are designed to use the least force possible to get potentially dangerous situations under control. With these rules in place, the damage to the parties should be minimized.

Unfortunately, many have learned conflict resolution with siblings where parents acted as referees to resolve the issues for you. There are no referees in marriage. When you have unresolved conflict in marriage, the only winner is Satan. "Us" loses. Be sure to learn how to master conflict resolution skills.

When you get into conflict with your spouse, how will you engage each other? Will you act out of anger or self-control? Will you seek your own needs over those of your spouse? Will you seek to protect your spouse? What will you do to love your spouse through the conflict? At the end of the day, what good is being "right" or "getting your way" at the expense of your marriage? You might "win the battle but lose the war."

There is great wisdom in agreeing how you will engage each other when you have conflict. Like the rules of engagement, having your plans spelled out will help to reduce the damage and create opportunities for resolution.

PREPARATION EXERCISES

Some rules to agree to ahead of time may be:

- Never go to bed mad.

- Never say the word "divorce" during an argument.

- Start all complaints with a prayer, an appreciation, and a suggested resolution.

- Resolve all conflicts with a kiss and a prayer.

- Don't use extreme words, such as "You always ..." or "You never ..."

- Give specific examples of what upsets you, not generalities.

- When your spouse is upset, agree to sit down with them face to face and actively listen to their concerns without defending yourself. After ensuring that you heard them correctly, then you can reverse roles for speaking and listening. The goal is understanding your spouse, not getting your point across.

- If you leave, let the other person know where you are going and how long you will be gone, and do not go for more than a short period of time (like an hour).

- No running home to Mama, unless you are in harm's way.

- Only refer to "you" when you are doing active listening in your reflective understanding of what the speaker is saying. For example, "You are saying that I upset you when I don't take out the trash."

THE CHRISTIAN PRENUPTIAL AGREEMENT

- When expressing anger, let your spouse know how you feel with statements like, "When you don't take out the trash, I feel unloved."

- Get to a counselor or mentor if you cannot resolve a serious conflict immediately.

Of course the best way to avoid conflict is to have good communication. There are great programs available to provide you with tools. Most premarital programs have training in building communication skills.

Ask ten couples who have been married for a long time what they do to keep their communication lines open. How do they avoid conflict? Add any new ideas on this list. Create your own "Rules of Engagement" and post them on your refrigerator. This will be a great reminder for you and a great learning tool for your children. After all, the best place for your kids to learn conflict resolution skills should be from you.

PREPARATION EXERCISES

What are our rules?

THE CHRISTIAN PRENUPTIAL AGREEMENT

Exercise 4

Writing Your Statement of Faith

Joshua speaking: *"Now fear the LORD and serve him with all faithfulness ... But if serving the LORD seems undesirable to you, then choose for yourselves this day whom you will serve" (Joshua 24:14a, 15a).*

The beginning of any agreement is understanding each other's purposes and motives. Are you a follower of Jesus Messiah? Do you pursue God daily and want to honor Him with your marriage? Is God on the throne of your heart?

Having a statement of faith helps ensure that your goals align, and it gives your children guidance to help them understand what you believe. Take time now to write your statement of faith. Start separately, and then share them. Work to create a joint statement of faith.

Creating your statement of faith provides a great opportunity to find out what your church believes. You may find that you are not in total agreement with your church, but it is a great starting point. It's also good to look at different church creeds, such as the Apostles' Creed or the Nicene Creed.

Some of the issues you may wish to address are:

• Are you Protestant or Catholic?

• Are you denominational or nondenominational?

• Do you believe in a triune God?

PREPARATION EXERCISES

- What do you believe about God, the Father?
- What do you believe about Jesus, the Son?

- What do you believe about the Holy Spirit?

- What do you believe about sin?

- What do you believe about salvation?

- What do you believe about baptism?

- What do you believe about the sacraments?

- What do you believe about communion?

- What do you believe about Mary and the virgin birth?

- What do you believe about gifts of the Spirit?

Attach this to your prenup or include its language within the context of it.

Here's a sample of what one might look like. This list is very generic in an attempt not to offend or dismiss any readers, but you may wish to make yours very specific — especially if you do not want your children to be raised in a particular type of church. Some issues are polarizing. For example, you may believe that speaking in tongues is a sign of salvation and want your child to be raised in a Pentecostal church or you may deny that tongues has a relevant place in the Christian world today and do not want your child raised in a Pentecostal church. This is your time to make a declaration of your beliefs. What you believe is foundationally important to your lives together.

THE CHRISTIAN PRENUPTIAL AGREEMENT

Sample Statement of Faith

- We are first and foremost Christians, without respect to denominations.

- We believe in the triune God: Father, Son, and Holy Spirit.

- We believe that God the Father Almighty created Heaven and earth and rules from His heavenly throne.

- We believe Jesus Christ is the only Son of the Father and is our Lord, Savior, and Master. We believe He was conceived by the Holy Spirit, was born of the virgin Mary, lived an earthly life healing and teaching, and ultimately suffered under Pontius Pilate, was crucified, dead, and buried. He descended into hell and on the third day He arose again from the dead and ascended into Heaven where He sits at the right hand of God the Father Almighty. From there He shall come to judge the living and the dead.

- We believe the Holy Spirit was given by God the Father Almighty to indwell the saints and convict us of our sins.

- We believe in the infallibility of the Word of God.

- We believe in the fellowship of believers through the Church.

- We believe in "believer's baptism" and will raise our children accordingly.

- We believe in the communion of saints.

- We believe in the resurrection of the body and the life everlasting.

PREPARATION EXERCISES

- We believe that we are sinners and that Jesus Christ came to pay our sin debt once and for all on the cross.

- We believe: For it is by grace you have been saved, through faith — and this not from yourselves, it is the gift of God — not by works, so that no one can boast (Ephesians 2:8-9).

THE CHRISTIAN PRENUPTIAL AGREEMENT

Exercise 5

Financial Planning

According to Dave Ramsey's Financial Peace University:

- 37 percent of marital problems derive from financial situations.

- 70 percent of all consumers live paycheck-to-paycheck, meaning they run out of money before the end of the month.

- The average family would have to use a credit card to pay a $1,500 unexpected expense (ex: home or car repair).

- Nearly half of all Americans (46%) have less than $10,000 saved for their retirement.[38]

Satan must be happy with these statistics. Money stresses and debt can be great tools in his hands to destabilize marriages. Surely this is why God mentions financial issues over 800 times in the Bible.

"No one can serve two masters. Either you will hate the one and love the other, or you will be devoted to the one and despise the other. You cannot serve both God and money" (Matthew 6:24).

PREPARATION EXERCISES

There is much you can do to combat the negative effects of finances on your marriage. Knowledge and planning are key.

First, it's imperative to recognize your financial compatibility. Are you a spender or a saver? How about your fiancé? It is not uncommon for couples to be opposites when it comes to finances.

It's also important to disclose your credit rating. I suggest that you each pull your credit reports and share them. The important thing is to recognize your tendencies with money, discuss them, and then implement a plan to deal with them.

One of the most effective ways to do this is to take a Crown Financial Ministries or Dave Ramsey Financial Peace University class together. Learning how to handle finances God's way will be the best investment of time and money that you can make in preparing for your marriage. Check with your local churches to find out who is hosting a class or go online to their websites to find out where the classes are being taught.

Otherwise, there are some things that you can do to head off financial problems and plan effectively for your marriage.

Budgets and Business Meetings

Sit down with your fiancé and map out your current income and spending. There are financial worksheets available online. They essentially start with your income — less withholding — to reveal your net income. Next, deduct your tithe. This is how much you have to spend. Note that this amount could be more or less if you adjust voluntary withholding amounts, like 401(k) savings. Then list what you spend money on, like housing expenses (rent, insurance, water, power, maintenance), vehicle expenses (car payments, insurance, gas, and maintenance), technology expenses (phones, data, computers), health costs (insurance, doctors), food costs (groceries, dining out), debt service (payments on loans and credit cards), vacations, recreation, personal care, and miscellaneous. You can get this information from your checkbook or credit card statements. (I was shocked at how much I was

THE CHRISTIAN PRENUPTIAL AGREEMENT

spending on cups of coffee at Starbucks and Dunkin Donuts, as well as beverages at restaurants. Between my husband and I we were spending over $1,200 per year just on dining out beverages.)

Combine your numbers based upon what you expect your incomes and expenses to be when you are married.

Talk about what you believe are extravagant or unnecessary on your own part. Talk about your goals for your finances. What kind of plans can you make to eliminate debt? Eye opening, isn't it? Use this information to determine what you need to include in your prenup.

Budgets and finances are fluid, so whatever you put in your agreement should allow for modifications. Having regular discussions to monitor how well you are doing with your budget and to set future monetary goals is critical to a healthy financial situation, and therefore, a healthy marriage.

Plan regular business meetings. They are not romantic, so pick a day of the week other than date night. You may want to have business meetings more often in the early days of your marriage until your finances are steady or until you have a good understanding of how decisions and spending are impacting you. Agree to do it away from children or other distractions. You may also want to agree to revise or renew your budget on January 1st of each year or a month after filing your income tax returns.

Bank Accounts and Saving for a Rainy Day

Separate bank accounts contradict the one-flesh doctrine. However, that does not preclude you from having multiple bank accounts to accomplish spending and savings goals. You may have a household account into which you deposit enough money to cover the monthly budget. You may wish to have an account in which you save up for replacement items, such as cars, roofs, appliances, etc. You may even wish to use an old-fashioned envelope system, where you put the money that is allocated for various parts of your budget into envelopes until it is time for the expenditure to be paid.

PREPARATION EXERCISES

Income

How much income do you need to earn and who is going to work? Are you planning for one to earn income and the other to be a homemaker or homeschooling parent? If so, is that permanent or is that if/when there are children at home?

Making a decision for a woman to be a homemaker has long-term ramifications. Either by death or divorce, she sacrifices a career that she may never be able to redeem. A couple may even be sacrificing a higher income if the wife earns more than the husband.

Start your marriage on the right foot. Analyze where you are financially and plan for your future, reflecting on what honors God and what produces your marital homerun.

"Do not store up for yourselves treasures on earth, where moths and vermin destroy and where thieves break in and steal. But store up for yourselves treasures in heaven, where moths and vermin do not destroy, and where thieves do not break in and steal. For where your treasure is, there your heart will be also (Matthew 6:19-21).

THE CHRISTIAN PRENUPTIAL AGREEMENT

Exercise 6

Keeping In-Laws from Becoming Out-Laws

* * * * *

The newlywed wife said to her husband when he returned from work, "I have great news for you. Pretty soon, we're going to be three in this house instead of two."

Her husband ran to her with a smile on his face and delight in his eyes. He was glowing of happiness and kissing his wife when she said, "I'm glad that you feel this way since tomorrow morning, my mother moves in with us."

* * * * *

There are two commands that we are called to obey with regard to parents and marriage: honor and leave.

> *"Honor your father and your mother, as the LORD your God has commanded you, so that you may live long and that it may go well with you in the land the LORD your God is giving you" (Deuteronomy 5:16).*

> *That is why a man leaves his father and mother and is united to his wife, and they become one flesh (Genesis 2:24).*

This is a tough balance. Getting your own new voice and establishing your own family is critical to the success of your marriage, and it is ordained by God. Even the best of parents may rebel and feel hurt when their opinion is no longer sought in the important decisions of your new life together. When you choose

PREPARATION EXERCISES

not to come to their house for a holiday, they may feel like you are being ungrateful when considering "all they have done for you."

In our wedding vows, we agree to forsake all others. This includes our parents. It means that we look wholly to our spouse for the issues of our lives. We value our parents' wisdom, but we ultimately rely on our spouse's opinion. We set our own new traditions and do not rely on how we were brought up as a basis for what we expect in our new "us." We love our parents, but we ask that they respect our new family.

I recommend two documents to help with this transition: A letter to your parents honoring what they have done in your lives and a parental commitment agreement so that they can agree to honor your new family. (I jokingly call this the Parental Non-Interference Agreement.)

Honoring Your Parents

Your parents have made your wedding day possible, if for no other reason than because they brought you into this world. For some, they will have participated in your lives in wonderful ways. For others, they may have passed away or perhaps you have strained relationships with them. Whatever the case, God used them to create you. It is important to always remember God's requirement to honor your parents.

I suggest that you do several things:

- Recognize whatever good they have done for you, like sending you to college, or pushing you to be a better person, or paying for the wedding.

- Recount any great memories of how they helped you become who you are.

- If they have been good role models, especially for marriage, recognize how that has counted in your life.

175

THE CHRISTIAN PRENUPTIAL AGREEMENT

- Acknowledge how hard it is for them to let you go and let you make your own new life and your own mistakes. Include Genesis 2:24.

- Present this letter at a special meeting, such as over dinner, just to honor them.

Parental Commitment (Non-Interference) Agreement

While honoring your parents, it is critical to your fledgling marriage to establish your new boundaries. Before you can do that, you need to know what you expect from each other in regards to family traditions and family relationships. Perhaps you could craft a side agreement about how you plan to deal with your parents that might look something like this:

In anticipation of our marriage, we agree that we will continue to love and respect our parents, but in a whole new way. God calls us to leave our parents and become one, which means that we will be starting our new family and our own family traditions. Each of us has had traditions in our own families. We agree to discuss those as they arise and then to make decisions about what we would like for our own traditions. We therefore agree to the following:

- We will honor and respect our parents in all ways. We will keep healthy boundaries with them, protecting our marriage from parental interference.

- We plan to spend holidays in our own home, unless we make special plans to be elsewhere. We will do our best to spend time with our families at the holidays, but will first establish our own new family traditions.

PREPARATION EXERCISES

- We will create our new family traditions for the holidays by discussing what we did in our homes and then deciding what we like and want to do in our own homes.

- We will attempt to include family in our holidays in a meaningful way, which may mean having dinners on the eves of the holidays or with them on the holidays, but we will not accept guilt from our parents if we do not spend holidays with them.

- We would prefer if our parents could babysit any future kids rather than babysitters, but will not put demands on them for this.

- We would love for our parents to be involved in our future children's lives to the greatest degree possible.

- We will spend our vacations alone unless there is a special occasion, such as a family reunion.

- We agree that family is important to us and to our future children. For this reason, we hope to stay within 50 miles of our families unless we are forced to move for a job. If that occurs, we will try to visit our families at least once each year if we can afford the trip without breaking our budget.

You may wish to get more specific than this, such as:

- We will spend Thanksgiving at alternating homes of our families, unless they don't offer, in which case we will have Thanksgiving at our house.

- We will spend Christmas Eve in church.

- We will spend Christmas morning at our house and then invite our parents for Christmas dinner in the afternoon.

THE CHRISTIAN PRENUPTIAL AGREEMENT

Communicating Your New Boundaries to the In-Laws

Once you have determined your boundaries, it is important to communicate them to your parents. Before you get married, invite your parents to meet with you in a quiet location, perhaps over a meal. I would suggest the following format.

- Start with prayer.

- Acknowledge your gratefulness for all they have done for you and how your life is better because of them.

- Ask them about what their early married life was like so that they might remember some of their own struggles with their parents.

- Ask them how they felt about their in-laws and what issues they had in their new roles apart from their parents.

- Ask them about horror stories you have heard about in-laws intruding into couples' lives and ask if they dealt with any of that.

- Ask them how they established healthy boundaries with their in-laws.

- Tell them how difficult you believe it will be to deal with your new God-ordained requirement to cleave and leave.

- Express concerns about conflicts that you perceive might arise, such as where you will spend Christmas or who babies will be named after.

PREPARATION EXERCISES

Most pastors require a certain number of meetings with the engaged couple. You might wish to have a meeting with the pastor and parents. Your pastor can emphasize God's plan for marriage and let them know that they will have new roles as they relate to parenting.

I originally had the idea that you could get your parents to sign an agreement, but a number of people suggested that it might hurt their feelings. So perhaps the agreement below might be a guide for you to use when you meet with them to ensure that you cover all the issues that may arise in your new relationship. You might also just show them this from your book and ask their opinion. Hopefully, you will be able to have this discussion without hurting their feelings.

If later you find that your parents are not respecting your boundaries, revisit the idea of a written agreement with them or a letter to them.

In anticipation of our son's/daughter's marriage, we recognize that he/she is entering into a new relationship and becoming one with his/her new wife/husband. We recognize that since the day he/she was born, we have been called to train him/her up to release him/her back into God's hands so that he/she may become a new creature in Him. We recognize now that he/she is honoring God in her new relationship with his/her future wife/husband.

We uphold the verse of Scripture that states:

> *For this reason a man will leave his father and mother and be united to his wife, and they will become one flesh (Genesis 2:24).*

We, therefore, release you to unite to your wife/husband to become a new person in Christ. In recognition of your new family, we agree to the following:

- We agree to uphold and defend your marriage in every way that we are able.

179

THE CHRISTIAN PRENUPTIAL AGREEMENT

- We agree not to criticize the ways that you do things when we disagree with them.

- We agree to honor and uphold the rules that our children have set up for their families and their households.

- We agree not to butt into your lives uninvited.

- We agree to give you advice when asked without expectations that you will follow it.

- We recognize that you will be creating new holiday traditions for your new family. We understand that you may have holidays at your home. We may invite you to holiday celebrations but we will have no expectations that you will be able to make it and will not hold it against you if you do not come.

- We recognize that you will be starting your own vacation planning and may not be spending vacations with us.

- We will be happy to babysit for you if and when children come along with appropriate notice and if it fits our schedule.

- We agree to pray for your marriage daily.

Whatever the outcome, be sure to honor your parents, but hold to your God-honoring boundaries so that you protect your spouse and your marriage from well-meaning, but often boundary-encroaching, parents.

PREPARATION EXERCISES

Our Leave and Cleave plans

THE CHRISTIAN PRENUPTIAL AGREEMENT

Exercise 7

Do You Really Mean "For Better or Worse"?

* * * * *

There are three rings involved in every marriage: first the engagement ring, then the wedding ring, and finally the suffering.

* * * * *

This is a joke my pastor recently told when he started a series on Genesis and marriage. Unfortunately, only a small percentage of married people report being "happily" married. Are you truly ready for the trials and disappointments that come from two sinners marrying?

A wedding videographer recently told me about a wedding where it seemed like the bride only repeated the good parts: "For better ... for richer ... in health ... in good times ... in joy ... in triumph." But what about the worse, the poorer, the sickness, the bad times, the sorrow, and the failure?

The following is a list of questions to ponder. Pray and ask God to reveal to you how deeply you are committed to your promises and what He desires for you. Share your answers with your fiancé. Do you have the same responses?

PREPARATION EXERCISES

What would you do if:

- Your spouse makes fun of you, belittles you in front of your friends, or complains about your habits in public?

- Your spouse refuses to help with chores that he/she agreed to do?

- Your spouse becomes disabled, cannot work, and requires your assistance for basic functions?

- Your spouse has an accident leaving him/her in a vegetative state?

- Your spouse becomes an alcoholic who cannot function at work or at home?

- Your spouse spends more than you make which ultimately causes you to file for bankruptcy?

- Your spouse develops a mental illness that causes him/her to be unsafe around your children?

- Your spouse has a sexually transmitted disease that he/she did not disclose prior to marriage?

- Your spouse joins the military without consulting you?

- Your spouse quits his/her job to accept a job that requires relocation without consulting you?

- Your spouse has a physical ailment that causes sterility?

THE CHRISTIAN PRENUPTIAL AGREEMENT

- Your spouse has a genetically transmitted deformity that could show up in your children that was not disclosed prior to your marriage?

- Your spouse is self-indulgent, spending large sums of money on extravagant clothes, body treatments, big toys, or recreational activities?

- Your spouse is nasty to your family?

- Your spouse has an affair that he/she calls off, and you believe there is true repentance?

- Your spouse has an affair that he/she refuses to call off?

- Your spouse is a kleptomaniac and you constantly find items around your home that you know were not purchased?

- You find out your spouse has saved over $100,000 in a secret bank account?

- Your spouse develops a permanent physical problem that prohibits him/her from being able to function sexually?

- Your spouse commits a crime?

- Your spouse becomes addicted to pornography?

- Your spouse is clumsy, constantly breaks things, and ultimately burns the house down by accident?

PREPARATION EXERCISES

- Your spouse becomes a workaholic and comes home after midnight every night?

- Your spouse demands sexual activities that you find distasteful or unbiblical?

- Your spouse is only concerned with satisfying himself/herself sexually?

- Your spouse goes out in public in what you consider to be shameful dress?

- Your spouse regularly belches or passes gas in public unashamedly?

- Your spouse develops a gambling addiction causing you to lose your house and cars?

- Your spouse refuses to have sex with you?

- Your spouse commits a crime and goes to prison for ten years?

- Your spouse develops Alzheimer's disease or has a brain injury and no longer recognizes you?

- Your spouse lies to you constantly?

- You find out that your wife had an abortion prior to marriage that has rendered her unable to conceive?

- Your find out your husband fathered a child that even he did not know about?

- Your spouse is physically abusive?

THE CHRISTIAN PRENUPTIAL AGREEMENT

- Your wife agrees to have children, but then you find out that she has been secretly taking birth control pills so she can continue in her career that she worked so hard for?

- Your husband promises to be the breadwinner so you can stay home with the children, but cannot keep a job?

- Your spouse goes away on weekends and refuses to explain his/her absence?

- You find out your spouse had a sexual relationship with your best friend prior to your marriage?

From the above list, does it matter that the problems are intentionally caused by your spouse, accidentally caused by your spouse, or that your spouse has no fault? Will any of these situations cause you to say that you will no longer love, honor, and cherish your spouse? Is there an escape clause in your vows?

Does it change your perspective if you consider your spouse as your mission field? Whatever they do, will you work to bring glory to God for their lives? How can God be glorified in each of these situations? God did not promise that marriage would be easy. You are promising to love your spouse for worse.

Can you trust God with all these situations? The suffering place is a learning place. We don't truly understand faith until we have been squeezed.

Not only so, but we also glory in our sufferings, because we know that suffering produces perseverance; perseverance, character; and character, hope. And hope does not put us to shame, because God's love has been poured out into our hearts through the Holy Spirit, who has been given to us (Romans 5:3-5).

PREPARATION EXERCISES

Satan is the one who opposes us. A marriage that continually strives for godliness is a fortification that Satan cannot penetrate. Sheep that are separated from the flock are easily overcome. Satan is happiest when he destroys homes because it is then when the sheep can be overcome.

This does not mean that you simply put up with miserable situations, but rather that you seek God's help and godly counsel from others. Loving your spouse does not mean being a doormat or an enabler, but it does mean seeking God in everything. God will bless that in His time and it will count for eternity.

There is a time for everything,
and a season for every activity under the heavens:
a time to be born and a time to die,
a time to plant and a time to uproot,
a time to kill and a time to heal,
a time to tear down and a time to build,
a time to weep and a time to laugh,
a time to mourn and a time to dance,
a time to scatter stones and a time to gather them,
a time to embrace and a time to refrain from embracing,
a time to search and a time to give up,
a time to keep and a time to throw away,
a time to tear and a time to mend,
a time to be silent and a time to speak,
a time to love and a time to hate,
a time for war and a time for peace.

What do workers gain from their toil? I have seen the burden God has laid on the human race. He has made everything beautiful in its time. He has also set eternity in the human heart; yet no one can fathom what God has done from beginning to end. I know that there is nothing better for people than to be happy and to do good while they live. That each of them may eat and drink, and find satisfaction in all their toil — this is the gift of God. I know that everything God does will endure forever; nothing can be added to it and nothing taken from it. God does it so that people will fear him (Ecclesiastes 3:1-14).

THE CHRISTIAN PRENUPTIAL AGREEMENT

Exercise 8

A Tale of Two Households

One of the most dangerous attitudes in preparing for marriage is worrying about protecting your self-interests. But Jesus' love for His bride was not about protecting Himself from suffering. It was about loving us sacrificially.

This book is designed to help you shift your paradigm for marriage from self-protection to selflessness and provision. Its goal is to take the focus off how your spouse will be behaving and help you to focus on your walk with God and how you can become holier. When you are right with God, then you can be useful to God and your spouse.

Unfortunately when we begin dealing with prenups, our focus tends to slip back to self-protection. It's hard to avoid this tendency because legal issues are usually framed with the notion of "what is fair?" However, as Christians, it's important for us to understand that Jesus did not seek fairness when He took our place on the cross.

To exercise your selfless muscles, read these two case studies about divorce. We will use the same fact pattern for each couple (Harry & Sally and Fred & Wilma). This is an important exercise because you are sinners and divorce can happen. There are three points that are worthy of notation:

1. Every story has two sides. No one is innocent in the breakdown of a marriage. Often it seems that one party has made an unconscionable choice. Unfortunately, it may be that the other person caused so much pain that the "guilty" party felt like they had no other choice. Both must make choices to honor God in their actions

PREPARATION EXERCISES

and responses. Sinning in reaction to sin is not the answer. Help is widely available in all situations.

2. An attitude of selflessness is a choice. In contrast, self-protection is a reaction. Choosing to love your spouse is a decision that you must make every day.

3. Ultimately, you have to trust God with the results. God is not putting you together so that you can mold your spouse into the person you want them to be or feel like they ought to be. Now is the time to recognize who your spouse is and trust God with them. God deals with each person separately.

Background for Both Cases

Both the bride and groom are 30ish. The groom is a marketing executive with an MBA working for a national company making $150,000 per year. The bride is a buyer for a regional grocery store chain making $90,000 per year.

Future Husband's thoughts prior to marriage:

I grew up in a home with Christian parents who had a few rocky years, worked through their problems, and have now been married almost 35 years. I have three younger siblings. My dad worked and my mom stayed home to raise us. We didn't have a lot, but we knew we were loved.

I want that for my family. My fiancée has a great job, and she really loves it. I know it will be a great sacrifice for her to give up her career. She had an unstable home life growing up, so I know she is afraid to give up her job. But I will always take care of her.

189

THE CHRISTIAN PRENUPTIAL AGREEMENT

Future Wife's thoughts prior to marriage:

My parents divorced when I was 10. My dad is a great dad, but he made a lot of mistakes. Because Dad didn't want to pay child support, he insisted that we live with him half of the time. That meant that we had to go back and forth between their households. That was awful. I would need things that were at my other house and would have to go without.

Mom had to move us several times because of money problems. One time she moved us in with one of her boyfriends, but that only lasted a few months.

She had to work hard to make ends meet. I went to work when I was fifteen to help Mom out. I tried to go to college but had to drop out.

I want the best for my kids. I always envied kids whose moms stayed home. My husband turned out great and his family is great. But I am fearful of quitting my job because I have worked so hard to get where I am.

My fiancé says he'll always take care of me, but my dad probably said that to my mom, too. I'm afraid to trust him.

After much discussion, both agreed that having a mother at home would be best for any kids that they might have. The man convinced the woman that he would love her and take care of her as long as he lived, and that she would never have to work again. Knowing she was fearful of the unstable life she had grown up with, he assured her that even if they did get divorced, he would give her their home and the kids would not have to do the two-home shuffle.

In researching the alimony and child support laws, the couple found out that without a prenup, in the event of divorce, alimony would be paid to the wife based on her needs and their marital lifestyle. However, alimony would be reduced by the wife's earning capacity. In other words, the court would determine what the wife could make and would "impute" that income to her regardless of whether she actually goes back to work. Furthermore,

PREPARATION EXERCISES

alimony would be paid to the wife for half the length of their marriage. For a couple married ten years, the wife would be entitled to five years of alimony.

For child support, the state uses a formula for determining child support. The husband's income for this calculation is based on his actual income less his alimony payments. The wife's income is based on the imputed income (whether actual or not) plus the alimony payments. The child support will be based on how many overnights the children are scheduled to spend with each parent (the closer to equal, the lower the child support).

For this couple, without a prenup, this most likely would mean:

- The wife would have income imputed to her at $90,000 per year, since that was what she earned most recently, regardless of her actual ability to get that job back or a similar one earning that pay.

- If the wife were awarded the marital home, she may not be able to afford it, and so the house may have to be sold.

- The children would most likely go to public schools, as opposed to homeschooling.

- The courts may have a presumption of equal timesharing or the husband may make a demand for equal timesharing for the purpose of reducing the child support.

- The children will most likely have to travel between homes on a court-ordered time-sharing schedule, which includes splitting holidays, vacations, and other events.

THE CHRISTIAN PRENUPTIAL AGREEMENT

After reviewing the state laws, the wife was even more fearful of giving up her job for the family. To assure her, they drafted a prenup in which the wife agreed to give up her career for kids and the husband agreed to support her for life, allowing her to keep their marital home in the event of divorce. (There were other provisions in case of disability or death.)

Case 1: Harry and Sally

Harry and Sally have now been married for ten years and have three children. According to plans, Sally is homeschooling their children. However, over the ten years Harry became a workaholic, often working late. Ultimately, Harry fell in love with his secretary and decided he wanted a divorce. Harry moved out and filed for divorce.

According to their prenup, Harry will support Sally and she will not have to return to work. She can continue to homeschool the children. Both Harry and Sally will have to live on less than half the total income and neither will have disposable income for investment, travel, or luxuries.

Is that the right outcome for Sally?
Is that the right outcome for Harry?

More Information

When Harry moved out, he moved in with his mistress. When he realized increased timesharing with the kids reduced child support, he demanded fifty percent timesharing. Harry began to feel the financial stresses of supporting two households and decided to fight the prenup. His former provider attitude disappeared and he moved into self-centered mode.

If the prenup holds, then Sally may be able to stay in the home instead of returning to work. However, the courts may not agree

PREPARATION EXERCISES

with their time-sharing arrangement and the amount of child support. The kids could potentially begin the two-house shuttle. That would mean that the children would be living with the woman who, in their eyes, stole their father away.

Is this the right outcome for Sally?
Is this the right outcome for Harry?
Is this the right outcome for the kids?

More Information

Up to now, Harry may seem like the villain. Would it change your mind if you found out that Harry behaved the way he did was because he felt like he was driven away or even hated in his own home? Over the ten years, Sally became resentful of having to stay home with the kids. She felt like she had to do everything because Harry was never home. She became contentious. Every day when Harry came home, she chided him for his inadequacies, and made him feel worthless. She even turned the kids against him. Going home was a living hell.

Over the years, she began to withhold sex from him as a weapon to get her way. Even when they did have sex, she let him know that she was doing it out of duty and just tolerating it. By the time ten years rolled around, they had not had sex for over two years. She refused to seek counseling and change her ways.

Is it any wonder that Harry began to work late to avoid going home? Unfortunately, he confided his troubles to his secretary who believed he walked on water. She could not believe that anyone would treat "Mr. Wonderful" in this manner. Neither of them intended for this affair to occur, it just did. (One of the most common slippery slopes to adultery is when spouses confide in coworkers of the opposite sex.)

Is Sally's contentious behavior an excuse for adultery? No. Harry should have sought counseling on his own. But it changes how you feel about Harry, doesn't it? Do you still believe that

THE CHRISTIAN PRENUPTIAL AGREEMENT

Harry should provide lifetime support for Sally or give her the house?

Case 2: Fred & Wilma

Fred and Wilma had the same family backgrounds, were the same ages, and had the same jobs as Harry and Sally. Over their first decade together, Wilma became an alcoholic. Fred often came home to find the house a mess, the kids running wild, and his wife drunk. The kids managed to get their homework done, but Fred suspected that his oldest was really helping fill in the gaps. After a trip to the emergency room for a health issue related to the alcoholism, Fred convinced Wilma to get help. Things got better for a while.

Then one day, Fred got a call from the police that one of the kids had set the garage on fire, but no one was hurt. Wilma was found unconscious as the result of a drinking binge. When Fred got home, his oldest child revealed that Wilma had been drinking because she had been dumped by her secret lover. Fred filed for divorce right away.

> Do you believe Fred should have filed for divorce right away or tried to work it out?
> Should Fred have to support Wilma for life?
> Should Wilma continue to stay at home to homeschool the children?
> Who should get custody of the kids?
> Should Wilma be able to keep the house?

Now take a step back from both these cases. Did you find yourself judging who was to blame or asking what's fair? Aren't those worldly mentalities? How does that fairness mentality align with vows to love "for better or worse"?

Choosing divorce is always self-centered. Staying married is a choice for your spouse. It does not mean that you stay in the same home with them if they are dangerous or that you enable their addictions. It also does not mean that you immediately take them

PREPARATION EXERCISES

back after they have repented of adultery. But isn't God honored if you continue to pray for them and leave a door open for God to heal the relationship or at least for them to be restored to the Kingdom?

Do nothing out of selfish ambition or vain conceit. Rather, in humility value others above yourselves, not looking to your own interests but each of you to the interests of the others (Philippians 2:3-4).

THE CHRISTIAN PRENUPTIAL AGREEMENT

Exercise 9

What Are You Going To Do about This?

In addition to the provisions suggested in the main text, there may additional topics for you to discuss so that you are like-minded when you marry.

False Expectations

Every couple brings false expectations with them to marriage. A husband may expect his wife to get up every morning and fix him breakfast because that's what his mother did. A wife may expect her husband to get up every Saturday morning to mow the lawn because that's what her father did. It's important to discuss family lifestyles — especially holidays — and how those existing traditions will be incorporated in your new family. You won't be able to anticipate them all, but an open discussion will help avoid conflicts.

PREPARATION EXERCISES

Church and Faith

- What church do you plan to attend and when?

- Do you share a faith and doctrine?

- What would keep you from attending church?

- What Bible classes will you take or lead?

- What ministry will you work in together/apart?

- Will you tithe? If so, how much?

- What evangelical organizations will you support?

- What do you believe about baptism?

- Do you believe that dancing is sinful?

- Do you believe that alcohol consumption is sinful?

- What plans do you have to be a witness for Christ?

- Do you plan to be a part of formal evangelism training or church visitation teams?

- What will you do to fulfill the Great Commission? (See Matthew 28:16-20.)

THE CHRISTIAN PRENUPTIAL AGREEMENT

Money

- Who is/are going to be the income provider(s) in your marriage?

- Can you live on one income?

- How much do you plan to save?

- Are you self-disciplined when it comes to money?

- Can you reconcile a checkbook?

- How do you track your finances?

- Will you use a budget?

- How much debt do you have?

- When do you want to retire?

- How much do you believe you need to have saved before retirement?

- Do you currently contribute to a 401k or other savings/retirement plan?

- What do you believe you will be earning in the career of your choice?

- Who do you believe will make the spending decisions?

- What purchasing decisions do you believe should be made jointly?

PREPARATION EXERCISES

- What purchasing decisions can each of you make independently?

- Is there a dollar amount over which you believe that you should not unilaterally decide to spend money?

- Who will pay the bills?

- Do you want to own a home or rent?

- Do you lease or purchase cars?

- When do you think it is appropriate to incur debt or use credit cards?

- Do you believe in debt for car purchases?

- Do you believe in mortgages to purchase homes?

  o If so, what do you believe is the appropriate period of time to pay off the loan?

- What charities do you want to support and how much do you want to give them?

- What are your spending policies for dining out, vacations, entertainment, hobbies, clothing, and personal services such as hair and nails?

- How often do you want to have business meetings to review spending, savings, and money planning?

- How often and when do you want to revise your budget?

THE CHRISTIAN PRENUPTIAL AGREEMENT

Sexpectations

- Have you agreed to abstain from sex until your wedding night?

- If you have not abstained from sex, will you abstain from sex until the wedding now?

- Do you intend to use birth control?

  o If so, what kind?

- Have you shared your sexual histories, including any abuse or abortions?

- How important is your achieving an orgasm?

- How important is your partner achieving an orgasm?

- Men, what will you do to help your spouse get in the mood?

- Ladies, what will you do to visually please your husband?

- Are there any forms of sex that you consider to be off limits?

- Are there any forms of sex that you consider to be sin?

- What is the maximum amount of time that you should go between encounters?

PREPARATION EXERCISES

- How will you let your spouse know that you are feeling sexually frustrated?

- Do you believe that sex is generally healthy during pregnancy?

- When do you believe it is appropriate to abstain from sex?

- What are your expectations regarding sexual satisfaction during times of unavailability due to medical reasons or physical absence, such as military duty?

- What will you do to keep the romance alive in your marriage?

- Do you have a preference on sleepwear?

- How do you feel about children in the marriage bed?

- How do you feel about cribs or bassinets in your bedroom?

- Have you agreed to keep pornography out of your relationship?

THE CHRISTIAN PRENUPTIAL AGREEMENT

Considerations for Virgins

- You may be fatigued on your wedding night from the day's activities. Would you consider holding off on sex until the following day?

- Have you met with a gynecologist to consider products and methods that might make your first encounter more pleasurable?

- Do you know what a hymen is and how to reduce the possible pain that may be associated with tearing or breaking it?

- Will you agree to be honest enough with each other to express your feelings, discomfort, or fatigue?

- What are you planning to do to relax before starting?

- Have you considered how to handle possible early ejaculation with your first encounters?

PREPARATION EXERCISES

Divorce Prevention

- Will you guard against things that can tear down your marriage such as pornography, soap operas, romance novels, television, or other societal poisons that can damage your marriage?

- Will you commit to do things to strengthen your marriage such as date night or attending marriage conferences periodically?

- Will you do team building activities, such as praying together, reading together, and Bible study?

- Will you commit to eating together around the table for most meals?

- Will you use outside resources such as mentors?

- Will you protect intimacy when children come along and promise to keep each other at the center of your marriage?

THE CHRISTIAN PRENUPTIAL AGREEMENT

Work

- Do you like your occupation?

- Would you like to change occupations? If so, when and how?

- Do you like your employer?

- Do you plan to stay with your employer?

  o If not, when do you plan to change?

- Do you like your boss?

  o If not, what are you going to do about it, if anything?

- What are acceptable occupations for each of you?

- What are your long-term goals for work?

- Do you both plan to work throughout your marriage?

  o If not, when do you plan to work?

- Do you plan to retire?

  o If so, when?

- Will you be agreeable to relocating if work requires it?

- What are acceptable work hours?

PREPARATION EXERCISES

- How do you define "workaholic"?

- What will you do if work begins to interfere with your marriage relationship?

- Do you find your significance in your position at work?

- Have you considered planning your budget so that you can live on one income?

THE CHRISTIAN PRENUPTIAL AGREEMENT

Time Off

- How do you like to spend your time off during the week?

- What recreational activities do you like?

- Do you believe in watching television?

  o If so, how much time is appropriate?

- Who will be in control of the TV remote?

- Do you like to read books?

  o If so, would you like to read books together?

- Do you enjoy playing cards or board games with each other and with friends?

- Do you like to read the newspaper or magazines?

  o If so, when?

- How much time do you spend on the computer reading news or surfing the web?

- How do you like to spend your vacations from work?

- Have you historically traveled to or with your family for your vacations?

  o If so, do you want to continue to do that?

PREPARATION EXERCISES

- Do you want to take vacations apart from children if/when you have them?

- Do you like to cruise?

- Do you like to camp?

- Do you like to travel internationally?

- What percent of your budget do you plan to spend on vacations?

- Do you want to own any recreational vehicles?

THE CHRISTIAN PRENUPTIAL AGREEMENT

Children

- How many children do you want to have and when?

- Do you want your sons circumcised?

- Will you use birth control?

  o If so, will you consider how the method works (i.e., whether it will destroy a fertilized egg)?

- If you have an "oopsie" baby, how will you adjust for that?

- Do you want to take in foster children?

- Do you want to adopt children if you cannot have your own?

- Do you want to adopt children in lieu of having your own, or some combination of your own and adopted?

- Will someone stay home with the children?

  o If so, to what age?

- Is spanking okay?

  o If so, to what age?

- Who will change diapers and get up in the middle of the night to feed and care for babies?

- Who will you allow to babysit?

PREPARATION EXERCISES

- What do you believe about early childhood schooling or daycare?

- Where do you want your children to be schooled — government, private, Christian, or home school?

- Do you anticipate schooling changes at different ages, such as homeschool until high school?

- Do you care if Christian schools are Protestant, Catholic, or Pentecostal?

- What if your children reach school age and you don't have the money to send them to private or Christian school?

- Will your children have allowances, and if so, will they have to earn them?

- What faith/denomination do you want your children to be raised in?

- What do you believe about baptism for your children?

- When will you pray with your children?

- Will you set up college funds for your children?

- What will you do if you cannot conceive?

- Would you like to be foster parents or adopt children?

- Will your work-life plans change if your children have special needs?

THE CHRISTIAN PRENUPTIAL AGREEMENT

Health

- How important is a healthy lifestyle to you?

- What is your target goal for number of hours of sleep?

- What will you do to ensure enough sleep?

- How much exercise do you need or want?

- How much exercise do you believe your spouse should have?

- Do you believe that you should belong to and work out at a gym?

- Do you believe that your spouse should belong to and work out at a gym?

- What is your weight goal for yourself and for your spouse?

- What will you do if you gain too much weight?

- What will you do if your spouse is overweight?

- What do you consider to be a healthy diet? (e.g. three meals? Meat eater? Soda drinker?)

- What foods do you not want in your house, such as junk foods?

- Do you have an eating disorder?

PREPARATION EXERCISES

- Do you have any health issues that require medical attention?

- Do you have any allergies?

- How often do you go to the doctor for regular checkups?

- How often do you get eye examinations or dental checkups?

- Do you believe in cosmetic surgery?

- Are you presently on any medications?

  o If so, what are they and what are they for?

THE CHRISTIAN PRENUPTIAL AGREEMENT

Personal Space

- What spaces in your home do you consider yours? (desk, garage, closet, chair)

- What spaces do you consider community space?

- Who is responsible for cleaning your personal space?

- If your fiancé moves your personal items from your personal space, how will you feel about that?

- Is there anything that you own that you would not like for your fiancé to touch, access, or change?

   o If so, what?

- Do you believe your fiancé makes good use of personal space? If not, where do you think he/she could improve?

PREPARATION EXERCISES

Stuff

- What furniture will you have in your home?

- Do you expect your fiancé to part with any of his/her furniture?

- Do you tend to keep things (pack rat) or get rid of things?

- If you are a pack rat, can you give up stuff that your fiancé thinks you will never need?

- If you like to get rid of things, can you allow your spouse to accumulate things in certain areas?

- What do you own that you would never give up?

- Who will decide how your home will be decorated?

- How do you store your financial records?

THE CHRISTIAN PRENUPTIAL AGREEMENT

Clothing and Grooming

- What do you believe is appropriate attire for going out in public, such as shopping or going out on a date?

- Do you believe that your fiancé is ever overdressed or underdressed in public?

  o If so, when?

- Have you agreed upon how much closet space each of you will have?

- Have you agreed upon how much drawer space each of you will have for clothing and grooming items?

- How often do you believe it is appropriate to shop for clothing?

- Do you believe that your fiancé has too many or not enough clothes?

- Do you believe in cutting and doing hair treatments at home or in a barber shop or hair salon?

- Do you believe in having regular manicures, pedicures, facials, or spa treatments?

  o If so, how often?

- Which of your fiancé's grooming habits do you believe are either overdone or need improvement?

PREPARATION EXERCISES

Chores

- Do you believe there should be a set division of duties for each of you around your home?

  o If so, what chores do you believe that each of you should do?

- If one of you is not working outside the home, does that change who is responsible for the chores?

- How do you believe that your upbringing has affected what you believe about chores?

- Do you agree with the way your fiancé keeps up his/her home now? If not, what do you believe they should change?

- Are there any chores that you refuse to do?

- Which of you likes to cook?

- Who will be responsible for the nightly meals at home?

- Do you believe in paying services to handle certain chores, like maid service or lawncare?

- Do you consider yourself neat or messy?

- Do you consider your fiancé neat or messy?

- If you are messy, do you plan to change or do you want your fiancé to accept your habits?

THE CHRISTIAN PRENUPTIAL AGREEMENT

- If you are neat, can you live with a messy person?

- Do you believe in using dry cleaning services?

  o If so, for what items and who will pick up/drop off laundry?

- Who has the ultimate decision in landscaping and lawn service?

PREPARATION EXERCISES

Etiquette and Manners

- Do you believe that your fiancé lacks manners in any area?

  o If so, where?

- Did your family have high expectations for etiquette?

  o If so, do you have those high expectations?

- What are your expectations regarding bodily functions, such as bathroom doors being open or shut, belching, and passing gas?

- Does your fiancé have any habits that you consider to be rude in public?

  o If so, what are they?

- Does your fiancé have any habits that you consider to be rude in private?

  o If so, what are they?

- What signal will you use to let your fiancé know that you find something rude when you are in public?

THE CHRISTIAN PRENUPTIAL AGREEMENT

Charitable Work

- What charitable work do you currently do?

- What charitable work do you plan to do once married?

- What charitable work would you like to do with your spouse?

- What charitable work will you involve your children in?

PREPARATION EXERCISES

Pets

- Did you grow up with pets?

- Do you want pets when you are married?

  o If so, what kind?

- Are there any animals that you will not have as pets?

- Are there any animals you fear?

THE CHRISTIAN PRENUPTIAL AGREEMENT

*THE CHRISTIAN PRENUPTIAL AGREEMENT*

Appendix

Additional Food for Thought

THE CHRISTIAN PRENUPTIAL AGREEMENT

Appendix Overview

Here Comes the Bridegroom

The Chemistry of Love

As It is Written, so Shall It Be Done!

What Is Divorce and Family Fragmentation Costing You?

Sample Christian Prenuptial Agreement

Here Comes the Bridegroom

Marriage is a beautiful expression of love that God gave us to better understand our relationship with Him. He uses marriage to describe the relationship He desires to have with us (His Church). Ancient Jewish marriage customs are a beautiful portrait of what Jesus has done, is doing, and will do in the future for us, His Bride.

In ancient times, the prospective bridegroom and his father would travel from their home to the home of the prospective bride. The bridegroom would request a daughter's hand in marriage from the bride's parents, and, if she agreed, they would negotiate the bride's price with her father. Once paid, the parents signed a prenuptial agreement (a ketubah) and the bride was set apart for the groom. While not yet married, they were considered husband and wife.

The betrothal period usually lasted a year, during which time the husband would return home to prepare an appropriate place for his bride. The wife would prepare herself physically, as well as preparing her wedding clothes or trousseau. During this time, even though the couple was considered married, they were not to have sexual relations.

At the father's appointed time, the bridegroom would depart his father's house with his groomsmen to fetch the bride. Because this period was generally a year, she knew approximately when he would be coming, but not the exact day or hour. The groomsmen would shout as they approached the bride's place to let her know of the groom's arrival. The bride would veil herself and, along with her attendants, would gather her things and return with the groom to the groom's father's house.

THE CHRISTIAN PRENUPTIAL AGREEMENT

The wedding party would be there waiting at the groom's house for their arrival. The couple would enter the Huppah (bridal chamber) alone. They would consummate their marriage covenant by entering into a physical union. The groom would announce the consummation to the best man, who in turn announced the news to the wedding guests.

Once the consummation was announced, a seven-day feast would begin, while the bride and groom remained protected in the wedding chamber for the duration. The groomsmen would stay posted at the door to be sure that the couple got whatever they needed while they were sequestered. At the end of seven days, the newlyweds would emerge with the bride unveiled for all to behold, joining the wedding feast with their guests.

Then for a year after the wedding, the husband was to stay home to bring happiness to his wife (Deuteronomy 24:5).

Jesus is the Bridegroom and we are His Bride. Jesus humbled Himself by leaving His heavenly Father's home to come to His Bride's house (earth). Donald Barnhouse suggested that God's proposal to us would go something like this:

> If you, Bride, will accept, "I, Jesus, [will] take thee, sinner, to be My Bride. And I do promise and covenant before God the Father and these witnesses, to be thy loving and faithful Savior before God the Father and these witnesses, to be thy loving and faithful Savior and Bridegroom; in sickness and in health, in plenty and in want, in joy and in sorrow, in faithfulness and in waywardness, for time and for eternity.[39]

When we accept Jesus' proposal, the covenant is sealed with His blood and we are set apart. He paid the bride price for us with His own death on the cross. We get baptized and begin the process

HERE COMES THE BRIDEGROOM

of sanctification to prepare for the wedding day. We prepare our wedding clothes.

For now, Jesus has returned to His Father for the period of separation (betrothal period) to prepare a place for us (John 14:1-3). Only the Father knows the exact day and time of His return (Matthew 24:36). When God releases Him to return, it will be with a shout (1 Thessalonians 4:16)! He will come with the Heavenly Host (His groomsmen) to gather us to Himself (Matthew 16:27-28) and take us into the Huppah for seven days after which we will be announced as His Bride to all and will be with Him forever.

Those who do not accept His proposal will be eternally separated from Him.

Have you accepted Jesus' proposal for eternal life? If you have not, now is a great time to do so. Recognizing that you do not deserve what He is offering you, and that He fully paid the price for your sins, repent of those sins. Repentance means that you recognize that you have sinned against God, acknowledge those sins, and make a U-turn away from them. Say "Yes" to Jesus, and He will sign the covenant, making you part of His Bride, the Church.

It is my prayer that I may count you as my brother or sister for eternity. It is the most important decision that you will ever or make. If you have more questions concerning this decision, be sure to discuss this with your pastor, or feel free to contact me via the website: www.christianprenup.com.

Blessings!

THE CHRISTIAN PRENUPTIAL AGREEMENT

The Chemistry of Love

God created us to be relational beings. He wired men and women differently. Those differences cause us to communicate, work, and play differently. It's almost as if we are aliens. (Thus the book, *Men are from Mars, Women are from Venus.*) Neither gender's characteristics are better, they're just different.

God created our bodies to produce certain neurochemicals, without which it is unlikely that we would choose to mate at all, much less with the aliens. We would most likely want to live our lives with someone who is like us. Thanks to God's design for our bodies' chemical reactions, we find ourselves at the altar promising to love an alien for the rest of our lives.

Neurochemicals are defined as "compounds forming largely in the brain and participating in neural activity."[40] There are a variety of neurochemicals that take us from puberty to *eros* love to *agape* love — all with the purpose of helping us form godly relationships and stay in them in a covenantal fashion.

While this section focuses on the chemical causation of attraction and attachment, there are other behavioral factors involved in human mating. For example, physical attractiveness, common life experiences, high comfort levels, pleasurable odors, and similar cultural backgrounds all play roles in what attracts us to another. Researchers even studied how eye contact with strangers can lead to infatuation.[41] Researcher John Money suggests that through your life experiences, you build a "love map" that causes certain factors to trigger the chemical reactions that lead to *eros* love.[42]

While behavioral experiences may lead us to be attracted, it is critical to understand the chemical forces that are unleashed when we begin to be attracted so that you are not surprised by the physical responses that you experience. Misuse of these chemicals is like playing with fire.

THE CHRISTIAN PRENUPTIAL AGREEMENT

Attraction Stage: Eros Love

God created our bodies to release certain chemicals at various stages of our lives to cause us to be attracted to each other. Being "in love" is a physical reaction to a number of neurochemicals. It is as if Cupid's arrow is dipped in "love drugs."

Hormones: Estrogen and Testosterone

God created two hormones that cause us to be men and women: testosterone and estrogen. While both men and women have some of each, women are marked by high levels of estrogen and men by testosterone. These hormones are present throughout our lives, but after puberty, these hormones create a desire to love that is not present in younger children. This is when the suggestion of playing with the opposite sex suddenly goes from "yuck" to "yeah."

Italian researchers found that when couples are in the initial stages of being "in love," men produce lower than normal levels of testosterone and women higher. The researcher, Donatella Marazziti of the University of Pisa, was quoted as saying, "Men, in some way, had become more like women, and women had become more like men. It's as if nature wants to eliminate what can be different in men and women, because it's more important to survive and mate at this stage."[43] (Of course, we know it's not "nature," but God who created us to draw closer.)

Attraction Neurochemicals

The body produces three neurochemicals that cause us to feel as if we are "in love": phenylethylamine, dopamine, and norepinephrine.[44]

> **Phenylethylamine** is the controlling agent for the release of the other two chemicals.

228

THE CHEMISTRY OF LOVE

Dopamine causes feelings of bliss. We also become more talkative and excitable.

Norepinephrine works like adrenaline to get the heart racing and the palms sweating. It also increases the experience of joy and reduces appetite.

The combination of these chemicals produces "elation, intense energy, sleeplessness, craving, loss of appetite and focused attention."[45]

Serotonin. Some researchers have found that people in love have lower levels of serotonin. Obsessive-compulsive people have low levels of serotonin, which may explain why we obsess when we are in love.[46]

Pheromones are chemicals excreted by the body that can induce chemical reactions in others. They are picked up in the olfactory glands of the recipient, and have been known to change behavior in the recipient, making them more receptive for attraction.[47]

Warning: Addictive Nature

Prescription drugs come with labels disclosing dangerous side effects that may make it unsafe to operate heavy equipment. What is more dangerous than choosing a life partner and the parent of your children when you are high? So here's the warning label for love drugs:

Warning: Love drugs are highly addictive. These drugs may impair your ability to discern. Do not make life decisions without consulting with wise counsel while under the influence of this medication.

THE CHRISTIAN PRENUPTIAL AGREEMENT

In a study by The State University of New York at Stony Brook, researchers studied the impact of MRI brain patterns of those in love. Study co-author Author Aron stated, "Intense passionate love uses the same system in the brain that gets activated when a person is addicted to drugs." You essentially become addicted to love like being addicted to a drug.[48]

A study by Helen Fisher, a biological anthropologist at Rutgers University, found that love is an addiction. She studied the MRI patterns of the couples who were in love and found higher activity in the parts of the brain that are associated with in cocaine and nicotine addiction. She also tested men and women who had broken up and found similar activity in those same brain centers when they viewed images of their exes. She noted that those are the same centers that record physical pain, distress, and attachment.[49]

The addictive nature of these drugs may cause you to bury your head in the sand when faced with relationship challenges. In essence, your fiancé is your drug supplier. As long as you have him/her, then you'll feel great. If you rock the boat, you may lose your source of happiness.

While you should be aware of the potential dangers associated with attachment neurochemicals, it is important that we thank God for them. Without them, you would likely have never been attracted to your fiancé to begin with.

Attachment Phase: Agape Love

God wants you to enjoy your marriage for your lifetime. When we marry and begin having sex, three new drugs are released in the body: oxytocin, vasopressin, and endorphins.[50]

Oxytocin is a bonding agent. It is produced in women when they nurse, which causes a woman to bond with her child. In women, it is produced when a woman has

THE CHEMISTRY OF LOVE

an orgasm. In men, it is released when they achieve an orgasm with the woman they love. You might call this God's superglue. If you have ever glued skin on skin with superglue, you know how good the hold is — pretty much permanent (unless you want to lose some skin). God intends for you and your spouse to be permanently bonded together.

Vasopressin gives us the desire to have life-long monogamous relationships. It also helps men to be more caring fathers.

Endorphins produce a general sense of well-being. They act in the same manner as opiates and are highly addictive. They are released during intimacy, orgasm, excitement, pain, and exercise. They help the body settle into a comfortable and constant relationship and help you stay in love.[51]

These three drugs are a gift to marriage because they kick in when we begin having sex (after marriage) when the attraction chemicals are beginning to wane — eighteen months to three years from first attraction. The good news is that research has shown that these drugs can continue to be produced through romantic encounters throughout your married life.

When you are first married, you will most likely find it hard to believe that sex can become routine, because it's all new and exciting. But when life and children happen, women especially find themselves feeling exhausted at the end of their days. Sex may seem more like work. That is why it is important to date your spouse and avoid routines in sex. Your goal should be to stimulate the drug production. For women, it may be candles, flowers, or special dinners. For men, it may be lingerie or variety in behavior. If you work at it and love your spouse, you can keep the love juices flowing.

THE CHRISTIAN PRENUPTIAL AGREEMENT

If you have had sex before marriage with your fiancé, then you have already chemically bonded. Premature bonding may be a hindrance to making rational decisions about your relationship. How likely are you to be thinking clearly about serious relationship issues if you are already glued together? It is important to separate physically from this point forward to help you to see things more clearly.

If you have had sexual relationships with others prior to your marriage, you have bonded and subsequently broken your bonds. Studies have shown that having multiple sexual partners reduces your ability to form a lasting bond in subsequent relationships, as oxytocin production is lower in women who have bonded with other men previously.[52] For example, when you apply a bandage, it sticks so well that removing it causes pain. If you try to reapply a used bandage, it barely sticks at all. The same applies to your bonding drugs. If you have had relations with others prior to marriage, it is important to deal with this in counseling. Don't sweep this one under the rug.

Research bears this out:

> Women who cohabit prior to marriage or who have premarital sex have an increased likelihood of marital disruption. Considering the joint effects of premarital cohabitation and premarital sex, as well as histories of premarital relationships, extends previous research. The most salient finding from this analysis is that women whose intimate premarital relationships are limited to their husbands — either premarital sex alone or premarital cohabitation — do not experience an increased risk of divorce. It is only women who have more than one intimate premarital relationship who have an elevated risk of marital disruption. This effect is strongest for women who have multiple premarital coresidental unions. These findings are consistent with the notion that premarital sex and cohabitation have become part of the normal courtship pattern in the United States.[53]

Using the Teachman study and a previous study by the Heritage Foundation,[54] The Social Pathologist blog post[55] created the following chart, which supports what is noted regarding the adhesion factor of oxytocin reduction in multiple sexual relations. The bar chart is from the Heritage Foundation. The Teachman statistics are the four data points.

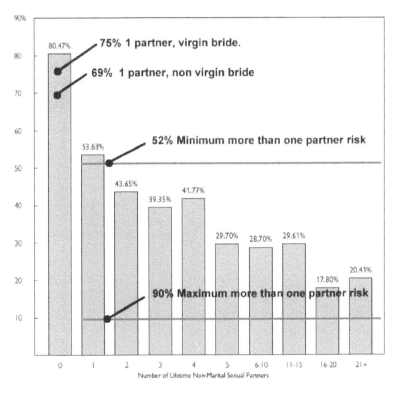

One additional admonition to consider concerning love drugs: There is some research being done to measure the possibility that viewing pornography also affects abilities to bond in marriage. One article, in fact, showed a downgrade in brain function from

THE CHRISTIAN PRENUPTIAL AGREEMENT

viewing pornography.[56] What have you decided to do to protect your marriage from the dangers associated with this addiction?

God created people with a beautiful operating system — a high performance machine. He gave us a user's manual (the Bible). When we do things according to God's owner's manual, we not only honor God, but we can achieve the joy that He intended for us to have.

As It Is Written, so Shall It Be Done!

Who can forget these words as spoken by Yule Brenner in the movie, *The Ten Commandments*? His powerful exclamation emphasizes that he means it. What does it mean when we put things in writing?

> *Jesus answered, "**It is written**: 'Man shall not live on bread alone, but on every word that comes from the mouth of God'" (Matthew 4:4, emphasis added).*

When God put things in writing, He indicated that truth was being spoken, and therefore it was important — you should sit up and take note. How important do you think the writing of the Ten Commandments is to God considering He wrote them with His own finger?

> *When the LORD finished speaking to Moses on Mount Sinai, he gave him the two tablets of the covenant law, the tablets of stone **inscribed by the finger of God** (Exodus 31:18, emphasis added).*

Blah, Blah, Blah ...

That's what we think about the spoken word. Unless it has been electronically recorded, the spoken word can be questioned later. It's only as good as the memory of the speaker and the listener (if they were listening). In courts of law, recounting what someone has said is called "hearsay" evidence and that type of evidence is

THE CHRISTIAN PRENUPTIAL AGREEMENT

often not allowed. Once something is in writing, it's hard to say, "That is not what I said."

Another problem with the spoken word is that we may not think about it when we say it or we may say things that we really don't mean. It's not uncommon to say things with good intentions, but later forget what you said or rationalize that you really didn't mean it that way. This was the premise of the opening chapter of the book, *Lies at the Altar*. The author, Dr. Robin L. Smith, presents a humorous, but unfortunately real, dialog of what a couple might really mean when they say their vows.

Good luck trying to enforce a spoken contract. It's "he said, she said," and is likely unenforceable by statute.

God's Emphasis on Writing

God made a number of covenants with us, His Church. By pressing Moses into the scribe service, God emphasizes how important it is for His Bride, the Church, to be on the same page with Him. To help us understand Him and to know how to be right with Him, God had Moses write the Pentateuch (known as the Torah in Judaism), which includes the first five books of the Bible. In these books we find the following:

- The history from the beginning
- The promises for the land, the seed, and the blessing given to Abraham
- The giving of the Ten Commandments
- The plans for the tabernacle
- The Book of the Law
- The Book of the Covenant
- The census at the beginning of the 40 years in the desert
- The census at the end of the 40 years in the desert
- The Song of Moses and Miriam (at the beginning of the 40 years)
- The Song of Moses (at the end of the 40 years)

AS IT IS WRITTEN, SO SHALL IT BE DONE!

Consider these other ways that God indicates the importance of the written word:

- The Bible is referred to as Holy Scripture. Scripture means writings.

- Jesus is the Word (John 1:1).

- God used the Jewish people to safeguard Scripture.

- Scribes (writers) were highly esteemed and agonized to get every jot and tittle correctly recorded. They were required to ceremonially cleanse themselves each time they wrote the name of Yahweh.

- Our names are written in the Lamb's Book of Life.

Accurate Understanding

An agreement is an acknowledgement of a fact or promise. A verbal agreement is only as good as the memories and desires of the parties and the witnesses. Recording an agreement helps ensure that all parties have an accurate understanding of what they are agreeing to. If the first draft does not properly convey the understanding, the document can be redrafted until all parties get on the same page.

The Bible calls us to be like-minded. Paul says it this way: having the same love, being one in spirit and purpose (Philippians 2:2). Often when we write an agreement, we find that there are elements that we have not previously discussed. Each of us may have had a different assumption about it, and we find ourselves disagreeing on this new element. Writing your plans and covenants helps you discover elements over which you might disagree and gives you the opportunity to become like-minded on these matters.

237

THE CHRISTIAN PRENUPTIAL AGREEMENT

Accountability/As a Witness between Us

> *"Come now, let's make a covenant, you and I, and let it serve as a witness between us" (Genesis 31:44).*

We often make rash agreements when we get caught up in the moment of an exciting time. After Moses had been on the mountain with God for forty days, he came down to the Israelites.

> *So Moses went back and summoned the elders of the people and set before them all the words the LORD had commanded him **to speak**. The people all responded together, "We will do everything the LORD has said" (Exodus 19:7-8a, emphasis added).*

The Israelites were quick to agree with what God told Moses to say. In the Law that Moses brought to them, God commanded no idol worship, and they agreed to obey God's Word. But when Moses left for another 40 days, they reverted to idol worship (Exodus 32). Clearly, man has a proclivity to put little weight on the oral promises. Thus, God had Moses write the Law.

> *After Moses finished writing in a book the words of this law from beginning to end, he gave this command to the Levites who carried the ark of the covenant of the LORD: "Take this Book of the Law and place it beside the ark of the covenant of the LORD your God. There it will remain **as a witness against you**. For I know how rebellious and stiff-necked you are. If you have been rebellious against the LORD while I am still alive and with you, how much more will you rebel after I die! Assemble before me all the elders of your tribes and all your officials, so that I can speak these words in their hearing and call the heavens and the earth **to testify against them** (Deuteronomy 31:24-28, emphasis added).*

238

AS IT IS WRITTEN, SO SHALL IT BE DONE!

Going from single life into married life is much like the Israelites going from forty years in the desert (our single life) into the Promised Land (marriage). We have had many idols in our desert. Often our greatest idol is us — seeking our own pleasures. God was calling the Israelites to leave their idols behind when they headed into the land of milk and honey.

Like the Israelites, we believe that once we get past the Jordan — or in our case, the altar — everything will be easy. But God knew better. In the Song of Moses (Deuteronomy 31:30–32:43), He told the Israelites they were sinners and were going to mess up and return to their old gods. And they did. Likewise, we are sinners. We fall into self-centeredness more often than we want to admit.

*The LORD said to Moses: "You are going to rest with your ancestors, and these people will soon prostitute themselves to the foreign gods of the land they are entering. **They will forsake me and break the covenant** I made with them. And in that day I will become angry with them and forsake them; I will hide my face from them, and they will be destroyed. Many disasters and calamities will come on them, and in that day they will ask, 'Have not these disasters come on us because our God is not with us?' And I will certainly hide my face in that day because of all their wickedness in turning to other gods.*

*"Now **write down this song** and teach it to the Israelites and have them sing it, **so that it may be a witness for me against them**. When I have brought them into the land flowing with milk and honey, the land I promised on oath to their ancestors, and when they eat their fill and thrive, they will turn to other gods and worship them, rejecting me and breaking my covenant. And when many disasters and calamities come on them, **this song will testify against them**, because it will not be forgotten by their descendants. I know what they are disposed to do, even before I bring them into the land I promised them on oath." So Moses wrote down this song that day and taught it to the Israelites (Deuteronomy 31:16-22, emphasis added).*

THE CHRISTIAN PRENUPTIAL AGREEMENT

Through these lessons, God makes it clear that we are sinners bent on self-centeredness. Furthermore, writing helps us to be accountable and is a witness to our covenant agreements.

Take to Heart

> *Moses came with Joshua son of Nun and spoke all the words of this song in the hearing of the people. When Moses finished reciting all these words to all Israel, he said to them, "**Take to heart** all the words I have solemnly declared to you this day, so that you may command your children to obey carefully all the words of this law. They are not just idle words for you — they are your life. By them you will live long in the land you are crossing the Jordan to possess" (Deuteronomy 32:44-47, emphasis added).*

> *The revelation from Jesus Christ, which God gave him to show his servants what must soon take place. He made it known by sending his angel to his servant John, who testifies to everything he saw — that is, the word of God and the testimony of Jesus Christ. Blessed is the one who reads aloud the words of this prophecy, and blessed are those who hear it and **take to heart what is written** in it, because the time is near (Revelation 1:1-3, emphasis added).*

When we were kids, if we wanted to make sure someone was telling the truth, we would make them swear the official kid's pledge: *"Cross my heart and hope to die."* What an awful expression. But what this expression emphasizes is that what is in our "heart" is our deepest desire. Likewise, we believe that if we put something in writing, we are taking it to heart.

AS IT IS WRITTEN, SO SHALL IT BE DONE!

Authority

Throughout the Bible, we find the words *"It is written."* The phrase is used to justify statements, words, or actions as being righteous — to be sure that they are pure and of God. For example,

> *"Afterward, Joshua read all the words of the law — the blessings and the curses — just as **it is written** in the Book of the Law" (Joshua 8:34, emphasis added).*

Now, let's consider when things aren't written. When Eve was in the garden, Satan came to her and questioned her about what God had instructed about the tree:

> *Now the serpent was more crafty than any of the wild animals the LORD God had made. He said to the woman, "Did God really say, 'You must not eat from any tree in the garden'?"*
> *The woman said to the serpent, "We may eat fruit from the trees in the garden, but God did say, 'You must not eat fruit from the tree that is in the middle of the garden, **and you must not touch it,** or you will die'" (Genesis 3:1-3, emphasis added).*

Eve did not have the written word. In fact, she may only have received the command not to eat from the tree from her husband. Having the command in writing would have allowed Eve to know what God said. God did not say, "You must not touch it." Eve (or Adam) added that to what God had said.

Satan twisted God's Word. *"Did God really say, 'You must not eat from any tree in the garden'?" (Genesis 3:3).* This question allowed Eve to doubt what God had said. Don't we do that when we want to rationalize bad behavior? We look for the out. Satan

THE CHRISTIAN PRENUPTIAL AGREEMENT

tempted her with the things that get us all: the desire to be more and have more, the desire to have control and power over our lives. R. C. Sproul coined a phrase that fits her act. She committed "cosmic treason."

Now contrast Eve's oral rationalization to what happened when Jesus was tempted by Satan in the desert. Using the same temptation for control and power, Satan offered Jesus power to meet His own needs and to be in control. What did Jesus say in His defense?

Then Jesus was led by the Spirit into the wilderness to be tempted by the devil. After fasting forty days and forty nights, he was hungry. The tempter came to him and said, "If you are the Son of God, tell these stones to become bread."

*Jesus answered, "**It is written**: 'Man shall not live on bread alone, but on every word that comes from the mouth of God.'"*

*Then the devil took him to the holy city and had him stand on the highest point of the temple. "If you are the Son of God," he said, "throw yourself down. **For it is written**:*

"'He will command his angels concerning you, and they will lift you up in their hands, so that you will not strike your foot against a stone.'"

*Jesus answered him, "**It is also written**: 'Do not put the Lord your God to the test.'"*

Again, the devil took him to a very high mountain and showed him all the kingdoms of the world and their splendor. "All this I will give you," he said, "if you will bow down and worship me."

*Jesus said to him, "Away from me, Satan! **For it is written**: 'Worship the Lord your God, and serve him only.'"*

Then the devil left him, and angels came and attended him (Matthew 4:1-11, emphasis added).

AS IT IS WRITTEN, SO SHALL IT BE DONE!

Jesus stood for righteousness and defended Himself with God's written Word. Perhaps your prenup will be the very document on which you will be able to take a stand for marital righteousness when you are fending off the attacks of the devil.

Planning Tool

One of the main goals of your prenup is to help you to understand each other's hopes and dreams so you will be headed toward the same destination. Working toward a common goal diminishes the chance of a couple "growing apart," which is the most common lament of couples divorcing today.

Building a marriage is similar to building a house. What do you want your house to look like? Would you build a house without building plans? Wouldn't your building plans be in *writing*? Would you build a house without a *written* estimate for the costs?

The plans of the diligent lead to profit as surely as haste leads to poverty (Proverbs 21:5).

"Suppose one of you wants to build a tower. Won't you first sit down and estimate the cost to see if you have enough money to complete it?" (Luke 14:28).

"A good plan is like a road map: it shows the final destination and usually the best way to get there."
— H. Stanley Judd

"Four steps to achievement: Plan purposefully. Prepare prayerfully. Proceed positively. Pursue persistently."
— William Arthur Ward

THE CHRISTIAN PRENUPTIAL AGREEMENT

But the noble make noble plans, and by noble deeds they stand (Isaiah 32:8).

It is rare for success to just happen. How much more likely are your plans to succeed if you put them in writing?

Measure of Performance

One of the greatest marketing tools that diet companies utilize is before and after pictures. When you record your expectations and goals for marriage, it sets a benchmark to measure how well you have done in attaining your goals. By comparing your expectations to your performance, you can make adjustments and work to make it better. You can stop, reflect, and ask yourselves, *"Have we honored God through our marriage?"*

God rescued the Israelites from slavery in Egypt, and they spent forty years in the Desert of Sinai. Because of their sin, God proclaimed that — other than Joshua and Caleb — not one man who entered the desert would enter the Promised Land. To prove His point He called for a census at the beginning of the forty years and at the end.

Beginning of the Forty Years

*The LORD spoke to Moses in the tent of meeting in the Desert of Sinai on the first day of the second month of the second year after the Israelites came out of Egypt. He said: "Take a census of the whole Israelite community by their clans and families, listing every man by name, one by one. You and Aaron are to count according to their divisions all the men in Israel who are twenty years old or more and able to serve in the army ... The total number was **603,550** (Numbers 1:1-3, 46, emphasis added).*

244

AS IT IS WRITTEN, SO SHALL IT BE DONE!

<u>End of the Forty Years</u>

> *After the plague the* LORD *said to Moses and Eleazar son of Aaron, the priest, "Take a census of the whole Israelite community by families — all those twenty years old or more who are able to serve in the army of Israel." ... The total number of the men of Israel was* **601,730** *(Numbers 26:1-2, 51, emphasis added).*

> *These are the ones counted by Moses and Eleazar the priest when they counted the Israelites on the plains of Moab by the Jordan across from Jericho. Not one of them was among those counted by Moses and Aaron the priest when they counted the Israelites in the Desert of Sinai. For the* LORD *had told those Israelites they would surely die in the wilderness,* ***and not one of them was left except Caleb son of Jephunneh and Joshua son of Nun*** *(Numbers 26:63-65, emphasis added).*

Forty years in the desert. Why did God call for a measurement at the beginning and the end of the journey? God knew His plans, and by documenting through a census, we are able to see that He is faithful to His Word. We can also see the impact of not upholding the covenant in a measurable way.

By measuring where you are at the beginning, you can see how far God takes you on your marriage journey.

As a Wave Offering

In the book of Leviticus, God commanded the people to present a wave offering to Him once they entered the Promised Land and annually in the spring after that. Perhaps your prenuptial agreement could be held up to the Lord as your wave offering each year as you celebrate your anniversary.

THE CHRISTIAN PRENUPTIAL AGREEMENT

The LORD said to Moses, "Speak to the Israelites and say to them: 'When you enter the land I am going to give you and you reap its harvest, bring to the priest a sheaf of the first grain you harvest. He is to wave the sheaf before the LORD so it will be accepted on your behalf; the priest is to wave it on the day after the Sabbath'" (Leviticus 23:9-11).

As a Symbol and a Remembrance

Hear, O Israel: The LORD our God, the LORD is one. Love the LORD your God with all your heart and with all your soul and with all your strength. These commandments that I give you today are to be on your hearts. Impress them on your children. Talk about them when you sit at home and when you walk along the road, when you lie down and when you get up. Tie them as symbols on your hands and bind them on your foreheads. **Write them on the doorframes of your houses and on your gates** *(Deuteronomy 6:4-9, emphasis added).*

God wants our love for Him inscribed (written) everywhere as a remembrance for ourselves and as a witness to others marking our covenant relationship with Him. How much does your prenup describe your covenant love for your fiancé?

Heritage

Can you imagine what the Baseball Hall of Fame would look like if statistics had not been kept on all the greats? What if there were no books written about the players ... no articles memorializing their stories and history ... no memorabilia? It would be a pretty empty building, would it not? By carefully recording the various aspects of a player's life, his story, his

AS IT IS WRITTEN, SO SHALL IT BE DONE!

memories, we can have a rich sports heritage that can be shared for generations.

Whatever you record prior to and during your marriage will be a living heritage that contains your hopes, dreams, plans, vows, and whatever else you put into writing. Documenting your prenup will be an encouragement to you as you encounter the valley experiences and learn how to walk through them. It will also be a treasure to your children when they embark on their own marriages.

Why in Writing?

The written word:

- Confirms that we are entering into a covenant with each other, and that we can hold this covenant up to God as a wave offering.

- Helps us to "take to heart" the agreement that we are making.

- Helps us to clarify our agreement.

- Can be revisited throughout the marriage as a reminder and a witness to what was promised.

- Can remind us of our sinful natures and help us plan ways to avoid broken promises. God knew that because we are a sinful lot, we would break our covenant with Him. But even so, He recorded in writing that He will never leave us or forsake us.

- Can be a legacy for our children to witness and possibly emulate when they are approaching their own marriages.

THE CHRISTIAN PRENUPTIAL AGREEMENT

It is my prayer that you will use your prenup as an opportunity to plan what honors God — with His glory being the focus of your plans.

May the God who gives endurance and encouragement give you the same attitude of mind toward each other that Christ Jesus had, so that with one mind and one voice you may glorify the God and Father of our Lord Jesus Christ (Romans 15:5-6).

What Is Divorce and Family Fragmentation Costing You?

This is an excerpt from an article that I wrote for the Good News Newspaper. (Reprinted with permission. Taken from the Good News in South Florida, August 2013. GoodNewsFL.org).

What happens when couples have healthy marriages? Couples are happier and healthier, live longer, are more financially stable, have better sex and intimacy, handle stress better, and raise children who have significantly better chances for success as they grow into adulthood. On the contrary, virtually every societal ill is rooted in the breakdown of the family.

Divorce rates have escalated over the last fifty years. Between 1960 and 2010, U.S. divorce rates have increased from 26% to 42%. Eleven of the 50 worst cities for divorce are found in Florida. This is how South Florida ranks:

Broward	64%
Miami Dade	68%
Palm Beach	67%

God's plan for marriage in America is not only fading, but is often mocked. America's new relationship norm is becoming co-habitation, out-of-wedlock childbearing and serial marriages. Consider that in the 1980s only 13% of the children of moderately educated mothers were born outside of marriage. In 2013, that has risen to 53%.

THE CHRISTIAN PRENUPTIAL AGREEMENT

Price Tag

The disappearance of healthy marriages costs us all. It is said, "Marriage is grand, but divorce is a hundred grand." Unfortunately, the costs of divorce reach far beyond the individuals involved. American taxpayers cough up $33.3 billion annually in social costs, which is in excess of $30,000 per divorce per year. When coupled with out-of-wedlock childbearing, the costs soar to $112 billion.

"Why Can't Daddy Live Here Anymore?"

Every day in Broward County an average of 22 couples are divorced, of which about half involve minor children. That translates to 11 parents explaining to twenty-something children daily (close to 150 kids weekly) that Daddy's not coming home.

The price tag for the kids?

- Nearly 40% of American children today live apart from their father. Fatherlessness is considered one of the most harmful demographic trends of this generation.
- Children raised by single parents are less likely to graduate from high school and/or be employed.
- Children raised by single parents are more likely to have delinquent behavior, get arrested, get pregnant, and have more mental health problems.
- Children living in homes with unrelated men are at much higher risk of childhood physical or sexual abuse.
- Children of divorce miss out on opportunities to develop critical relationship skills that are more likely to be modeled by parents in a stable marriage.
- Children raised in single-parent homes are five times more likely to be poor. 80% of long-term poverty occurs in single-parent homes. In 2008, 36.5% of single mothers were poor, compared to only 6.4% of married couples with children.

WHAT IS DIVORCE AND FAMILY FRAGMENTATION COSTING YOU?

Is There Hope?

Divorce rates can be changed by changing a culture. The question is: who is intentionally working toward change? Jesus said, *"The thief's purpose is to steal and kill and destroy. My purpose is to give them a rich and satisfying life" (John 10:10, NLT).*

Satan (the thief) has been destroying families by whispering the lie into our hearts and souls that marriage doesn't matter. By manipulating media and our school systems, Satan has convinced us that "It's all about me." Heard any of these?

- Sex outside marriage is okay. Just protect yourself.
- Oral sex isn't sex.
- Test drive your marriage ... live together first.

The good news is that, through education, we can learn to spot the lies, just as tellers at banks are trained to identify counterfeit money by studying what makes it counterfeit. A number of organizations have taken up the cause. Many of these have teamed up to form NARME (National Association of Relationship and Marriage Education). Research studies show clear evidence that relationship and marriage education (RME) programs work to reduce strife, improve communication, increase parenting skills, increase stability, and enhance marital happiness.

The saddest words spoken in divorce recovery classes are, "If I had only known ..."

Help stop the cycle of family fragmentation. Get involved in rebuilding America from the ground up.

THE CHRISTIAN PRENUPTIAL AGREEMENT

Sample Christian Prenuptial Agreement

WARNING: This is not intended to be a template for your prenup. It is for demonstrative purposes only to help you to understand certain concepts. Consult with an attorney to draft your agreement.

THIS AGREEMENT MADE IN TRIPLICATE THIS 1st day of January, 2014

BETWEEN:

HARRY SMITH
Of the City of Hope
In the State of Happiness

-AND-

SALLY JONES
Of the City of Hope
In the State of Happiness

<u>**PRENUPTIAL AGREEMENT**</u>

RECITALS

A. A Prenuptial Agreement is made between HARRY SMITH, hereinafter referred to as Prospective Husband, and SALLY JONES, hereinafter referred to as Prospective Wife, who are contemplating marriage to each other;

THE CHRISTIAN PRENUPTIAL AGREEMENT

B. The Prospective Husband acknowledges that the Prospective Wife has a dependent child from her previous marriage, namely JOHNNY JONES, JR, born in 2000; and further, that the son resides solely with the Prospective Wife, and that she receives no child support for her son;

C. The Prospective Wife acknowledges that the Prospective Husband has two emancipated children from his previous marriage, Harry Smith, Jr. and Harriette Smith Williams.

D. The parties intend for this Agreement to become effective upon their marriage solemnization pursuant to the laws of the State of Happiness;

E. The parties both profess that they are Christians, which they define as people who have put their faith in the Lord Jesus Christ and His saving grace, having accepted the free gift of eternal life with Him, having confessed their sin nature and repented of their sins, and who pursue His holiness in their lives. The parties agree with and have signed a statement of faith which is attached hereto;

F. The parties acknowledge that God ordained marriage such that, when a man and woman enter the Holy Estate of Matrimony, they shall leave their parents and cleave to each other, becoming one flesh according to Genesis 2:24;

G. The parties recognize God as their ultimate authority and place Him as head of their marriage. As such, the parties acknowledge the laws and precepts of the Bible as the authority and guidance for how their marriage will be governed. To wit:

1) The parties recognize that the Prospective Husband will be head of the Prospective Wife, and as such:

a) is called to love her sacrificially, as Jesus loved His Church and died for her while we were yet sinners;

b) is called to be a gentle master, as Christ is to the Church (not demanding, but loving);

c) is called to be a servant leader, as Jesus served His disciples;

SAMPLE CHRISTIAN PRENUPTIAL AGREEMENT

d) is called to be provider and protector of the family;
e) is called to submit to God, as Jesus submitted to God in His sacrifice on the cross;
f) is called to be responsible for the actions of his family; and
g) is called to love the Prospective Wife.

2) The parties recognize that the Prospective Wife will submit to her Prospective Husband, and as such:

a) is called to respect the Prospective Husband as head of the family, as Jesus is head of the Church;
b) is called to be nurturer of the family and provide counsel to the Prospective Husband; and
c) is called to support the Prospective Husband and be a help-mate so that together they can accomplish their godly pursuits.

H. The parties acknowledge that God calls them to love, which is defined as follows:

> *Love is patient, love is kind. It does not envy, it does not boast, it is not proud. It does not dishonor others, it is not self-seeking, it is not easily angered, it keeps no record of wrongs. Love does not delight in evil but rejoices with the truth. It always protects, always trusts, always hopes, always perseveres. Love never fails (1 Corinthians 13:4-8a).*

I. The parties acknowledge that God created sex for pleasure, for procreation, and to bring glory to Himself by celebrating marital oneness. They further acknowledge 1 Corinthians 7:3-5, which states that husbands and wives are not to withhold their bodies from each other sexually, as their bodies do not belong to them, but to their spouses, except for a time of prayer, after which they are to reunite with their spouses.

J. The parties acknowledge that marriage is not a 50%-50% partnership, but rather a relationship where both parties work toward maintaining a God-honoring household. This includes both parties sharing in the work of maintaining the household.

THE CHRISTIAN PRENUPTIAL AGREEMENT

K. The parties wish to enter into this Agreement to provide for the status and ownership of property between them, including future property to be acquired by each or both of them;

L. The parties wish to enter into this Agreement to provide for the status of income earned between them;

M. The parties acknowledge that both are currently working full-time jobs (the Proposed Husband as a realtor and the Proposed Wife as a CPA). Their incomes have been disclosed in the attached financial statements.

N. The parties further wish to affix their respective rights and liabilities that may result from this relationship;

O. The parties have exchanged financial statements providing full and complete disclosure of substantially all of the assets and property now owned and the liabilities now owed by each of them and voluntarily and expressly waive any other rights to disclosure of property or financial obligations of each other beyond the disclosure provided;

P. The parties acknowledge that they are both bringing debt into the marriage. The parties further acknowledge that debt is a master (Proverbs 22:7) and as such is to be avoided.

Q. The parties have prepared a prospective mutual budget based on their exchanged financial statements that includes a plan for debt extinguishment.

R. The parties acknowledge that God hates divorce, and only specifically allows divorce when one of the parties has committed adultery or when one of the parties is not a believer and leaves his/her believing spouse. Further, the parties acknowledge that even so, God does not require divorce, but only allows it because He knows our hearts are hard (Matthew 19:8);

SAMPLE CHRISTIAN PRENUPTIAL AGREEMENT

S. The parties acknowledge that the Bible commands Christians to make every effort to live at peace and to resolve disputes with each other in private or within the Christian Church as per 1 Corinthians 6:1-8 and Matthew 18:15-20.

T. The parties recognize that they are both sinners as described in the Bible in Romans 3:23: *for all have sinned and fall short of the glory of God.* Because of their sin nature, they acknowledge the possibility that one or both of them may seek a divorce, whether justly or unjustly. Accordingly, the parties desire that they that they will be governed by the terms of this agreement, and, insofar as the statutory case law permits, intend that, if the statutes contradict their Agreement, either by virtue of Federal or State legislation, the statues will not apply to them;

U. Each party has had the opportunity to receive counsel from a pastor or minister of the Gospel of Jesus Christ and receive independent spiritual counseling regarding the terms of this Agreement;

V. The parties acknowledge that they have completed premarital counseling courses in preparation for their marriage;

W. Each party has had the opportunity to retain their own lawyer and receive independent legal advice regarding the terms of this Agreement;

X. The parties have exchanged their medical and sexual histories providing full and complete disclosure of substantially all of their medical procedures, treatments, and known medical conditions and sexual relations.

Y. The parties acknowledge that they have been provided with a reasonable period of time to review this Agreement and obtain spiritual and legal advice before signing;

Z. Each party affirms the following:

1) THAT the parties did execute the Agreement voluntarily;

THE CHRISTIAN PRENUPTIAL AGREEMENT

2) THAT this Agreement was not unconscionable when this Agreement was executed;

3) THAT both parties were provided prior to the execution of this Agreement fair and reasonable disclosure of the property or the financial obligations of the other party; and

4) THAT he or she did have, or reasonably could have had, an adequate knowledge of the property or financial obligations of the other party.

NOW THEREFORE in consideration of the upcoming marriage, the aforementioned recitals, God's laws, and the mutual promises and covenants contained in this agreement, the parties agree as follows:

1. The parties agree to take each other as their lawfully wedded Husband/Wife.

2. The parties agree to love, honor, respect, trust, cherish, encourage, and support each other according to God's Holy ordinance.

3. The parties agree to stay married for better or worse, for richer or poorer, in sickness and in health, in good times and in bad, in joy and in sorrow, in failure and in triumph, until death parts them.

4. The parties agree to forsake all others and keep themselves only unto each other. To this end, they agree to:

   a. Leave their parents in accordance with Genesis 2:24 and look only unto each other for emotional, spiritual, and financial support, while still honoring their parents and respecting them for their positions in their lives;

   b. Avoid intimate conversations or confiding relationships with the opposite sex to avoid forming inappropriate relationships;

   c. Refrain from viewing pornography; and

   d. Not withhold sex from each other according to 1 Corinthians 7:3-5, except for times of mutual consent or illness. If one party requests an activity which may be deemed to be

SAMPLE CHRISTIAN PRENUPTIAL AGREEMENT

unconscionable, unhealthy, or pornographic, the couple agrees to seek and attend counseling from a pastor or Christian counselor for activities that one party may feel is unconscionable or pornographic or to seek a medical doctor if the activity is deemed to be unhealthy within 15 days of the parties' last sexual encounter. Both parties agree to work to satisfy the other party sexually, whether that is by romance or by visual stimulation. The parties agree to communicate their concerns and issues to the other at a time other than during a time of intimacy.

5. The parties agree to exchange and wear their wedding bands as a sign of their marriage to one another.

6. The parties agree to set a regular date night each week that they agree not to miss except for extreme cases of illness or other unavoidable event. The initial date night for the parties shall be Saturday nights, but may, by mutual consent, be changed to a different night of the week.

FINANCES

7. In accordance with God's one-flesh doctrine as described in Genesis 2:24, the parties agree to endow to each other all their worldly goods. All property shall be presumed to be jointly owned as by the entireties and all income shall be presumed to be jointly earned. The parties agree to work together to retitle all property within thirty days of their date of marriage.

8. The parties agree to assume joint liability for the debt of the other party according to the one-flesh doctrine and according to the pattern of Jesus assuming our sin debt on the cross.

9. The Proposed Husband shall strive to be the continual provider of income, and shall strive to work full time to support the family.

10. Because the Proposed Wife's child is fifteen years old, except as provided below, it is agree that the Proposed Wife will continue

THE CHRISTIAN PRENUPTIAL AGREEMENT

to work full-time, unless and until such a time as the parties may have other children, adopt other children, or provide foster care for other children, at which time the Proposed Wife may reduce or eliminate her job so that she may care for and nurture any future children.

11. The parties agree that tithing is the first charge against their monthly income and shall be paid before any other expenses. The parties agree to tithe 10% of their gross income to their church, unless mutually agreed upon to be tithed to another organization.

12. The parties agree to have a business meeting to discuss the finances and their schedules at least monthly to ensure that they are striving toward their budget goals and allocating their time in a God-honoring way. The initial day for these meetings is the first Tuesday of each month, which may be changed to a different day by mutual consent.

13. The parties agree to revise and/or renew their budget annually on January 1st of each year, with a goal of eliminating debts and investing in the Kingdom and investing for retirement.

14. In the event of illness or job loss, the parties shall work together to take up each other's roles until such a time as the illness or job loss can be remedied, with a goal of the Proposed Husband being the provider and the Proposed Wife being the mother/nurturer of the children.

15. The parties agree to make charitable donations in excess of their tithe to strategically support pro-life, evangelism, marriage education, and missionary organizations.

16. The parties agree that they will work together toward the investment goals established in their monthly budget, as attached hereto, and as amended on an annual basis at their January 1st meeting.

17. The parties agree that they will maximize the retirement programs offered by employers, or in the alternative, maximize their IRA contributions to the extent allowed by law, as a priority over

SAMPLE CHRISTIAN PRENUPTIAL AGREEMENT

discretionary expenses as detailed in their budget as attached and as amended at their January 1st meeting each year.

18. The parties agree to pay down their debts with a goal of extinguishing all debt according to the monthly budget that they have established together prior to entering into this agreement and as amended on their January 1st meeting each year.

19. The parties agree to discontinue use of credit cards until the balances are paid in full, after which time, the parties may again return to utilizing their credit cards, but agree to pay off their credit card balances in total monthly by the due date. In the event the parties cannot pay a credit card balance in total for any two consecutive months, the parties agree to cancel their credit cards for a period of one year after the balance is paid off, at which time they may reopen their accounts or apply for new credit cards.

CHILDREN

20. The Proposed Husband agrees to treat the Proposed Wife's child as his own and to provide support for him so long as he is a minor or graduates high school, whichever is later. The Proposed Wife agrees to treat the Proposed Husband as her son's own father.

21. The parties agree that they wish to help the Proposed Wife's child with college, but will make choices as to how that will be accomplished based upon ability and upon the child's dedication to his school work.

22. The parties agree that they wish to take in foster children as the Lord provides. They further agree that they may wish to adopt foster children as the Lord directs.

23. All children of the marriage, including the child of the Proposed Wife and any children that the couple may bear, foster, or adopt, will be raised according to the Christian faith. As such, both parties will encourage the children to accept the Lord Jesus Christ as their personal Lord and Savior and will encourage them to be baptized as

THE CHRISTIAN PRENUPTIAL AGREEMENT

soon as they make a genuine profession of faith. Further, both parents will strive for regular church attendance together as a family at least weekly.

24. The parties agree that Christian education is fundamental for their children's Christian foundation. As such, the parties agree to either homeschool in a Christian curriculum or send their children (whether natural, fostered, or adopted) to Christian schools. By Christian education, the parties agree that it must be Protestant and fundamental in nature, aligning with the statement of faith that the couple signs with this agreement.

25. The parties agree to assign chores to the children to which they must be held accountable, and at an age approximating sixteen years old, the children must seek outside employment to earn money to help provide for their spending and savings for college.

26. The parties agree to have family dinners at the dinner table at least five nights per week. The parties further agree to include at these dinners appreciations for each other, followed by sharing new information, schedules, and events. The parties may, by mutual consent, alter this schedule, but will in all circumstances, strive to keep the family connected through these meetings.

MARITAL HOME

27. The parties agree that they will initially establish the Prospective Wife's home as their marital home, and will strive to pay the mortgage on the marital home at twice the monthly payment as is feasible. Based upon the currently agreed upon budget, which includes this provision, this plan is feasible.

28. The parties agree to maintain a home within fifty miles of their mothers' retirement communities so long as their mothers shall live. After such time, the parties agree to discuss the possibility of moving as they feel led by God.

29. The parties agree to work together to maintain the family home. Neither party will be responsible for specific chores, and both will

SAMPLE CHRISTIAN PRENUPTIAL AGREEMENT

work toward a common goal of honoring the Lord with their home. Generally, the Proposed Wife shall be responsible for the housekeeping or overseeing the housekeepers and shall engage the children to assist to the greatest extent possible for them to gain life skills. Further, the Proposed Husband shall be responsible for the maintenance of the garage, the camper, the exterior house care, or overseeing the workmen who may do work around the home and shall engage the children to assist to the greatest extent possible for them to gain life skills.

OTHER PROPERTY

30. The parties agree that they will put the Prospective Husband's condo on the market for sale and sell it for a price that is not less than what he originally paid for it. Otherwise, they will hold the condo until such a time as the market returns and they can sell it at that price. They agree that they will attempt to rent it if it does not sell within a year, but only then will they rent it on an annual basis and not a shorter term.

31. The parties agree to sell their timeshare or otherwise work to eliminate it from their budget.

SEPARATION

32. The parties agree to live together in the Holy Estate of Matrimony and that, except as provided below, will not separate except for possible temporary circumstances, such as work, military service, or endangerment.

33. In the event of abuse, addiction, or adultery, the parties agree to separate immediately for safety and/or healing. The party involved in the abusive, addictive, or adulterous activities shall agree to vacate the marital home until such a time as it is deemed appropriate by mental healthcare providers to reenter the home. Both parties agree to seek Christian counseling by a licensed mental health counselor together and apart as recommended by the mental health professional. The parties will work together to keep the marital home intact if possible, especially for the sake of any dependent children.

THE CHRISTIAN PRENUPTIAL AGREEMENT

34. In the event of separation, neither party will attempt to interfere with the children's Christian faith, Christian church attendance, or school routines.

35. The parties recognize the authority of the court to determine what arrangements are in the best interests of the children, and understand that court orders may affect the arrangement of the parties as stated in this agreement.

DIVORCE

36. The parties agree not to use violation of the terms of this agreement as a basis for filing for divorce.

37. The parties agree that they will not file for divorce except as a last resort and as is biblically allowed; and even in those circumstances, will not proceed to a legal solution until the following steps have been taken toward reconciliation in this order:

    a. Notify and meet with their pastor immediately upon recognition of the problem that could lead to the divorce;
    b. Seek counseling together with a local licensed Christian mental health counselor;
    c. Follow the steps provided in Matthew 18:15-17, including bringing the dispute to the elders of the church;
    d. Attend a Christian marriage intensive weekend designed to restore marriages which are in distress; and
    e. Wait at least two years from the time of the first meeting with a pastor upon the notification of marital problems, whether jointly or separately.

38. In the event of adultery, addiction, or abuse, the parties agree to a waiting period of no less than two years before seeking a divorce to allow time for God's restoration, during which time the parties shall seek reconciliation as per above, including, but not limited to, counseling and marriage intensive weekends. The two-year period shall start upon the written confirmation of knowledge or acknowledgement of the adultery, addiction, or abuse. If the party or parties at fault are unrepentant, the other party will continue to honor

SAMPLE CHRISTIAN PRENUPTIAL AGREEMENT

God in their actions. The parties will work together to maintain the marital home during this period, except as the actions of one party are found to be unsafe, in which case the parties are to separate, as per above.

39. In the event that one of the parties files for divorce, based upon 1 Corinthians 6:1-8, the parties agree to the following:

    a. To uphold the provisions of this agreement to avoid unnecessary litigation over property division and support;
    b. To utilize Christian collaborative law attorneys if they need assistance with completing their marital settlement agreement as an alternative to full blown litigation;
    c. To utilize Christian litigation attorneys if their attempts at collaborative law do not prevail;
    d. That the Prospective Husband shall provide for the payment of attorney's fees, unless the Prospective Wife is committing adultery or abandons the marriage;
    e. To use only Christian attorneys so as not to violate the instructions of 1 Corinthians 6:1-8;
    f. To seek whatever alternatives allowed to having an ungodly judge preside over their divorce proceedings (to the extent that they exist), such as an Christian arbitrator or a Christian private judge who will agree to be bound by both God's laws and precepts where it is not precluded by secular law; and
    g. That under no circumstances will the parties seek a secular court to resolve their dispute except as required by law for the dissolution proceedings.

40. In the event of divorce, neither party will attempt to interfere with the children's Christian faith, Christian church attendance, or school routines. Further, neither party will expose the children to activities which are antithetical to the Christian faith, such as, but not limited to, anti-Christian music or movies, foul language, pornography, alcohol, illegal drugs, or fornication by the spouse with an unmarried partner, including the spouse living with an unmarried partner. Such activities will be cause to return the children to the other party until such a time as those activities can be eliminated from the children's environment. Even so, the parties will work toward having God-honoring time with the children.

THE CHRISTIAN PRENUPTIAL AGREEMENT

41. In the event of divorce, the Proposed Husband agrees to provide for the Proposed Wife as follows:

    a. Except as follows, the Proposed Husband desires and promises to support the Proposed Wife until death. By support, the Proposed Husband intends for the Proposed Wife to maintain their marital residence. The following exceptions apply:

        i. If the Proposed Wife has been contributing income to the family in the three-year period immediately preceding the divorce action, then his support shall be reduced proportionately based upon her contribution percentage to the household income;

        ii. If the Proposed Wife is involved in an adulterous affair, then the Proposed Husband is under no obligation to support the Proposed Wife, except to the extent that he may wish to provide support to maintain the household for any children of the marriage;

        iii. If the Proposed Wife is involved in addictive behavior and unable to maintain the marital residence, the Husband shall be under no obligation to maintain the support of the home, but instead may support the Proposed Wife's efforts to rehabilitate from the addictions according to her desire;

        iv. If the Proposed Wife enters any post-marital co-habiting relationship with another man, then the Proposed Husband shall be under no obligation to support the Proposed Wife; and

        v. If the Proposed Husband cannot work or has reduced income for reasons outside his control, then the Proposed Husband, except as provided above, will share his income with the Proposed Wife to the extent that the Proposed Wife does not receive from the Proposed Husband more than 50% of the total income earned by both parties.

    b. The Proposed Wife does not contemplate supporting her husband, nor does the Proposed Husband contemplate the Proposed Wife's support, except if the Proposed Husband becomes disabled in some fashion, such as by accident, physical illness, or mental illness, the Proposed Wife agrees to support the

SAMPLE CHRISTIAN PRENUPTIAL AGREEMENT

Proposed Husband to the greatest extent possible until death, or the husband remarries or enters another substantially supportive relationship.

ESTATES AND TESTAMENTARY DISPOSITION

42. The parties acknowledge that upon the death of either party, the other party shall be sole beneficiary of the deceased's estate, except as provided below.

43. The parties recognize that the Proposed Wife has a revocable living trust that names her son as sole beneficiary of her estate. The Proposed Wife agrees to amend her trust document within thirty days after the wedding to recognize the Proposed Husband as the sole beneficiary, except as provided below.

44. The parties agree to maintain life insurance valued at $200,000 on the life of the Proposed Wife for at least as long as the Proposed Wife's son is under the age of 25. The Proposed Wife shall change the beneficiary of the policy to name her Proposed Husband as the sole beneficiary. If the Proposed Wife predeceases the Proposed Husband, then the proceeds from the life insurance shall be set aside in the form of a trust for the maintenance and education of the Proposed Wife's son, including, but not limited to, college. The Proposed Husband shall be named trustee of said trust. Upon the son completing his education, or when the son reaches the age of 25, whichever is later, a remainder amount of $10,000 (or to the extent that any funds remain if it is less than $10,000) shall go to the son, with any other remaining funds going to the Proposed Husband. The Proposed Husband shall, at his discretion, determine the amount of maintenance for the son.

45. Except as provided for above, the parties agree to maintain life insurance policies for both parties with a face value of $200,000 for as long as is mutually agreeable to assist with the payoff of any mortgages and burial expenses.

46. The parties agree that in the event of either party's death, the other party shall pay to the deceased party's children over the age of 25 the

amount of $50,000 each and will give to those children any memorabilia that was acquired prior to the parties' marriage and relevant to the children that the remaining party deems reasonable. Further, because the remaining party will need to support themselves and may remarry in the future, there will be no further expectations for bequests of the former marital estate to the deceased party's children. The remaining party is free to grant additional bequests at their discretion.

47. In the event that the parties decease simultaneously or in close proximity of time such that the estate of the first to decease has not settled, then the total estate shall be divided into equal parts per stirpes among the three natural children of the former marriages, and any future natural or adopted children of the contemplated marriage. That is, if the parties adopt an additional child once married, their mutual estate would be divided in four parts or per stirpes to those children's lineal descendants.

SEVERABLITY

48. Should any portion of this Agreement be held by a court of law to be invalid, unenforceable, or void, such holding will not have the effect of invalidation or voiding the remainder of this Agreement, and the parties agree that the portion so held to be invalid, unenforceable, or void, will be deemed amended, reduced in scope, or otherwise stricken only to the extent required for the purposes of validity and enforcement in the jurisdiction of such holding.

INTENTION OF THE PARTIES

49. Notwithstanding that the parties acknowledge and agree that their circumstances at the execution of this Agreement may change for many reasons, including but without limiting the generality of the foregoing, the passage of years, it is nonetheless their intention to be bound strictly by the terms of this Agreement at all times.

SAMPLE CHRISTIAN PRENUPTIAL AGREEMENT

DUTY OF GOOD FAITH

50. This Agreement creates a fiduciary relationship between the parties in which each party agrees to act with the utmost of good faith and fair dealing toward the other in all aspects of this Agreement.

FURTHER DOCUMENTATION

51. The parties agree to provide and execute such further documentation as may be reasonably required to give full force and effect to each term of this Agreement.

TITLE/HEADINGS

52. The headings of this Agreement form no part of it, and will be deemed to have been inserted for convenience only.

EFFECTIVE DATE

53. This agreement shall be binding upon the parties upon the solemnization of their marriage according to the laws of the State of Happiness.

ENUREMENT

54. This Agreement will be binding upon and will enure to the benefit of the parties, their respective heirs, executors, administrators, and assigns.

GOVERNING LAW

55. The laws of the State of Happiness will govern the interpretation of this agreement, and the status, ownership, and division of property between the parties wherever either of them may from time to time reside.

THE CHRISTIAN PRENUPTIAL AGREEMENT

TERMINATION OR AMENDMENT

56. This Agreement may only be terminated or amended by the parties in writing signed by both of them.

IN WITNESS WHEREOF the parties have hereunto set their hands and seals as of the day and year first written above.

SIGNED, SEALED, AND DELIVERED

In the presence of:

_____   _____

Witness   Harry Smith

Printed Name:

_____

_____   _____

Witness   Sally Jones

Printed Name:

_____

Sources

Ananthaswamy, Anil. (May 5, 2004). Hormones converge for couples in love. *New Scientist Online Magazine.* Retrieved November 27, 2013, from www.newscientist.com/article/dn4957-hormones-converge-for-couples-in-love.html#.UpX8ik2A270

Atomic Scale Design Network. (n.d.). Chemistry of love. *ASDN.net.* Retrieved November 27, 2013, from www.asdn.net/asdn/chemistry/chemistry_of_love.shtml

Barnhouse, Donald G. (1961). *God's freedom.* (p. 191). Grand Rapids, MI: Ms. B. Erdmans Publishing Company. Cited in Showers.

BBC News. (June 14, 2004). Science proves that love is blind. *BBC News.* Retrieved November 27, 2013, from http://news.bbc.co.uk/2/hi/health/3804545.stm

Bray, Llona, J. D. (n.d.). Penalties for committing immigration marriage fraud. *Nolo.com.* Retrieved November 30, 2013, from www.nolo.com/legal-encyclopedia/free-books/fiance-marriage-visa-book/chapter1-9.html

Brown, Kathryn. (July 31, 1999). Love sick. *New Scientist.* Edition 2197. Retrieved December 30, 2013, from http://community.fortunecity.ws/underworld/continue/56/lovesick.html

Buzzle. (March 27, 2004). The chemistry of love. *Buzzle.com.* Retrieved November 27, 2013, from www.buzzle.com/editorials/3-27-2004-52238.asp.

The Church of England (1662). The form of solemnization of matrimony. *Book of Common Prayer.* Retrieved December 30, 2013, from www.pemberley.com/janeinfo/compraym.html

THE CHRISTIAN PRENUPTIAL AGREEMENT

Cleave. [Def. 1]. (2001-2013). Testament Hebrew Entry for Strong's #1692 – Cleave. *Studylight.org*. Retrieved December 30, 2013, from www.studylight.org/lex/heb/hwview.cgi?n=1692

Common law marriage. [Def. 1]. (1990). *Black's Law Dictionary*. p. 227. 6th ed.

Eggerich, Emerson, Ph.D. (January 1, 2008). Love and respect. *Love and Respect Video Course*

Entitleitis. [Def. 1]. (1999-2013). *Urban Dictionary*. Retrieved September 25, 2013, from www.urbandictionary.com/define.php?term=entitleitis

Fisher, Helen E. (April 1, 1992). The biology of attraction. *Psychology Today*. Sussex Publishers, LLC. Retrieved November 27, 2013, from www.psychologytoday.com/articles/199303/the-biology-attraction

Fraiman, Stephanie. (March 7, 2013). TheKnot.com and WeddingChannel.com reveal results of largest wedding study of its kind, surveying more than 17,500 brides. *Yahoo Finance*. Retrieved November 29, 2013, from http://finance.yahoo.com/news/theknot-com-weddingchannel-com-reveal-141000109.html;_ylt=AwrNUbBozzhRqEUALuDQtDMD

Gordon, Lori H. and Albertson, Richard. (n.d.) How do people learn?. *Adventures in Marriage Workbook, Christian Version*. (v.3.8), p.10.

Gungor, Mark. (March 16, 2009). The damage of sexual promiscuity. *Laugh Your Way to a Better Marriage*. Retrieved December 30, 2013, from www.laughyourway.com/blog/the-damage-of-sexual-promiscuity/

Haiman, Peter Ernest, Ph.D. (n.d.). Protecting a child's emotional development when parents separate or divorce. *PeterHaiman.com*. Retrieved November 30, 2013, from www.peterhaiman.com/articles/protecting-a-childs-emotional-development-when-parents-divorce.shtml

SOURCES

Harms, Roger W., M.D. (n.d.). Abortion: Does it affect subsequent pregnancies? *Mayo Clinic Staff*. Retrieved November 26, 2011, from www.mayoclinic.com/health/abortion/AN00633

The Heritage Foundation. (June 23, 2003). The harmful effects of early sexual activity and multiple sexual partners among women: a book of charts. *The Heritage Foundation*. Retrieved December 30, 2013, from http://s3.amazonaws.com/thf_media/2003/pdf/Bookofcharts.pdf

Heussner, Ki Mae. (July 8, 2010). Addicted to love? It's not you, it's your brain. *ABC News*. Retrieved November 27, 2013, from http://abcnews.go.com/Technology/addicted-love-brain/story?id=11110866

Hilton, Donald, Jr., M.D. (Summer 2010). Slave master: How pornography drugs & changes your brain. *Salvo*. Ed 13. Retrieved December 30, 2013, from www.salvomag.com/new/articles/salvo13/13hilton.php#sthash.VSZYhGOO.dpuf

Jacob, Rabbi Louis. (n.d.) The ketubah or the marriage contract. *My Jewish Learning*. Retrieved December 29, 2013 from http://www.myjewishlearning.com/life/Life_Events/Weddings/Liturgy_Ritual_and_Custom/Ketubah.shtml

Kim, Christine. (September 22, 2008). Academic success begins at home: How children can succeed in school. *The Heritage Foundation*. Backgrounder #2185 on education. Retrieved September 25, 2013, from www.heritage.org/research/reports/2008/09/academic-success-begins-at-home-how-children-can-succeed-in-school.

Koco.com. (February 6, 2013). Oklahoma covenant marriage bill approved in Senate Committee. *Koco.com*. Retrieved December 30, 2013, from www.koco.com/news/politics/Oklahoma-covenant-marriage-bill-approved-in-Senate-Committee/-/9843896/18431282/-/uygnbxz/-/index.html

Maltby, Anna. (July 2012). The benefits of being married. *MensHealth.com*. Retrieved December 30, 2013, from

THE CHRISTIAN PRENUPTIAL AGREEMENT

www.menshealth.com/mhlists/benefits_of_marriage_and_commitment/index.php

Mote, Edward. (Circa 1834). "My Hope is Built." *Hymns of Praise.* Retrieved September 25, 2013, from http://cyberhymnal.org/htm/m/y/myhopeis.htm

Obringer, Lee Ann. (February 12, 2005). How love works. *HowStuffWorks.com.* Retrieved December 30, 2013, from http://people.howstuffworks.com/love.htm

Ramsey, Dave. (n.d.). What does the Bible say about money? *Dave Ramsey's Financial Peace University.* Retrieved December 3, 2013, from https://crc.daveramsey.com/index.cfm?event=dspPastorExt&intContentID=10320

Reagan, Michael. (n.d.). Defending families against forced no-fault divorce. *marysadvocates.org.* Retrieved January 1, 2014, from www.marysadvocates.org/michaelreagan.html

Scofield, C. I. (November 1, 2011). The book of Ephesians. *Biblical Covenants.* Retrieved December 30, 2013, from www.ancientpath.net/Bible/NT/49_NewEphesians/Appendicies/49_eph_BiblicalCovenants_Scofield.htm

Showers, Dr. Renald. (n.d.). Jewish marriage customs: Behold, the bridegroom comes! Retrieved December 30, 2013, from www.biblestudymanuals.net/jewish_marriage_customs.htm

Slaughter, Anne-Marie. (July/August 2012). Why women still can't have it all. *The Atlantic.* Retrieved September 25, 2013, from www.theatlantic.com/magazine/archive/2012/07/why-women-still-cant-have-it-all/309020/

The Social Pathologist. (September 16, 2010). Sexual partner divorce risk. *The Social Pathologist.* Retrieved December 30, 2013, from http://socialpathology.blogspot.com/2010/09/sexual-partner-divorce-risk.html

SOURCES

Social Security Administration. (n.d.). *What is the best age to start your benefits?* Retrieved December 30, 2013, from www.socialsecurity.gov/retire2/otherthings.htm

Stewart, Rebecca Felsenthal. (n.d.). Does a better relationship mean better health?: The perks of marriage and long-term relationships. *webmd.com*. Retrieved from www.webmd.com/sex-relationships/guide/relationships-marriage-and-health

StrongerMarriages.org. (n.d.). Time, sex, and money: The first five years of marriage. *StrongerMarriages.org*. Retrieved December 3, 2013, from http://strongermarriage.org/htm/divorce-remarriage/time-sex-and-money-the-first-five-years-of-marriage

Tartakovsky, Margarita. (2012). History of psychology: How a marshmallow shaped our views of self-control. *Psych Central*. Retrieved on November 24, 2013, from http://psychcentral.com/blog/archives/2012/05/22/history-of-psychology-how-a-marshmallow-shaped-our-views-of-self-control/

Teachman, Jay. (May 2003*)*. Premarital sex, premarital cohabitation, and the risk of subsequent marital dissolution among women. *The Journal of Marriage and Family*, Vol 65, Issue 2, Pages 432-443.

Thomas, Gary. (2000). *Sacred marriage: What if God designed marriage to make us holy more than to make us happy?*. Grand Rapids, MI: Zondervan.

Thrasybule, Linda. (February 13, 2012). Falling in love affects brain much like addiction, scientists say. *Huffington Post*. Retrieved November 27, 2013, from www.huffingtonpost.com/2012/02/13/falling-in-love-triggers-brain-changes_n_1273196.html

Tompor, Susan. (Posted May 25, 2013). Will you marry me (and my student loan debt)?. *USA Today*. Retrieved December 3, 2013, from www.usatoday.com/story/money/columnist/2013/05/25/student-debt-marriage-wedding-loans/2351405/

THE CHRISTIAN PRENUPTIAL AGREEMENT

Acknowledgments

This book could not have been completed without the love and support of so many who helped me birth this project, especially the attorneys who helped guide me with the legal issues, and my friends who actually took the time to read the draft and give me feedback on the manuscript. There were so many, so if I missed anyone, please know that you helped to provide resources to further the Kingdom of God.

Holly Anderson
Theresa Taylor Berger
Grif Blackstone (Blackstone Media)
Karla Blake
Joanne Brown
Susan Brown, Esq.
Pastor Mark Burkey
Grace Chavis (great champion of marriage)
Ted Copella
Jeannette Coury (best mother in the world)
Philip & Katie Coury (best kids in the world)
M. Glenn Curran, III, Esq.
Cindy Daigle
Jane Davell (proofreader par excellence)
Bill Dunmeyer
Dr. Phillip Dunn
Guitry Gachelin
Dr. Warren Gage
Jim Geiger, Esq.

THE CHRISTIAN PRENUPTIAL AGREEMENT

Jan Gold
Laurin Greco (editor)
Rev. J. Patrick Hartman (husband extraordinaire)
Mark Grand, Esq.
Sandy Haduck
Perry Hodges, Esq.
Kary and Pat Johnson
Ollie Jolly
David Kofsky, CPA
Brian MacClugage
Peggy Madonna
Katie Randall
Doug Reynolds, Esq.
Joe Samaritano
Bill Shannon
Anita Smith
Roberta Stanley, Esq.
Pastor Fred & Barbara Steen
Misty Weinger, CPA
Dr. Norm Wise
Karen Zann, Esq.
Guy in the Dallas airport
South Florida Word Weaver's group

Author Bio

Patricia Hartman, CPA/ABV/CFF, CVA, CFE

- Shareholder and vice-president of Kofsky, Hartman & Weinger, PA in Hollywood, Florida
- Licensed in Florida as Certified Public Accountant
- Primarily performs forensic litigation services for clients going through divorce, as well as fraud examinations, business valuations, tax consulting, and business consulting
- B.S. University of Virginia 1979
- B.A. Florida Atlantic University 1998
- Twenty-five years in family and marriage ministries in South Florida, including premarital, marriage, divorce, and single parents
- Featured marriage and family writer for *The Good News in South Florida* newspaper
- Currently or previously certified instructor/facilitator for various marriage programs, including:
    - Start Smart Premarital Program®
    - Adventures in Marriage®
    - DivorceCare®
    - Our Home Runs
    - Marriage Links™
    - W.A.I.T (Why Am I Tempted?)
    - P.I.C.K. A Partner™/How to Avoid Falling for a Jerk(ette)™
- Author of *A Funny Thing Happened on My Journey to Heaven*
- Member of National Association of Relationship and Marriage Education (N.A.R.M.E.)
- Volunteer at the Lord's Gift House at First Baptist of Pompano Beach
- Member of the Single Mom's Advisory Committee of Sheridan House Ministries

THE CHRISTIAN PRENUPTIAL AGREEMENT

Endnotes

[1] "Forensic" refers to being an expert in a field who uses scientific or other acceptable methodologies to investigate legal problems and report them to the clients, attorneys, and/or the court. For divorce, the problem is determining income, expenses, assets, and liabilities. Not surprisingly, when couples go through divorce, parties often try to reduce their required amount of support by understating their income. They may also try to understate their assets to reduce the amount they have to give up when the marital estate is divided. As a forensic CPA, I am, in essence, a financial detective.

[2] The gravity of this section, along with the disclaimers that I offer throughout the book, should be a dead giveaway that I work in a legal environment. It seems like we have to put disclaimers on everything we do. Even as a CPA, we have to give a Circular 230 disclaimer when discussing tax matters. Ah, the world we live in and the stories I could tell — maybe I'll tell a couple in this book.

[3] See Preface for description of forensic.

[4] Gordon, Lori H. and Albertson, Richard. (n.d.) How do people learn? *Adventures in Marriage Workbook, Christian Version.* (v.3.8), p.10.

[5] M. Glenn Curran, III is a Martindale-Hubbell A.V. rated Preeminent Attorney who practices law in Fort Lauderdale, Florida, with the Curran Law Group.

[6] See "Here Comes the Bride" in the Appendix for more details on this relationship.

[7] Jacob, Rabbi Louis. (n.d.) The ketubah or the marriage contract. *My Jewish Learning.* Retrieved December 29, 2013 from http://www.myjewishlearning.com/life/Life_Events/Weddings/Liturgy_Ritual_and_Custom/Ketubah.shtml

[8] BBC News. (June 14, 2004). Science proves that love is blind. *BBC News*. Retrieved November 27, 2013, from http://news.bbc.co.uk/2/hi/health/3804545.stm

[9] Mote, Edward. (Circa 1834). "My Hope Is Built." *Hymns of Praise*. Retrieved September 25, 2013, from http://cyberhymnal.org/htm/m/y/myhopeis.htm.

[10] Entitleitis. [Def. 1]. (1999-2013). *Urban Dictionary*. Retrieved September 25, 2013, from www.urbandictionary.com/define.php?term=entitleitis

[11] Tompor, Susan. (May 25, 2013). Will you marry me (and my student loan debt)?. *USA Today*. Retrieved December 3, 2013, from www.usatoday.com/story/money/columnist/2013/05/25/student-debt-marriage-wedding-loans/2351405/

[12] StrongerMarriages.org. (n.d.). Time, sex, and money: The first five years of marriage. *StrongerMarriages.org*. Retrieved December 3, 2013, from http://strongermarriage.org/htm/divorce-remarriage/time-sex-and-money-the-first-five-years-of-marriage

[13] Tartakovsky, Margarita. (2012). History of psychology: How a marshmallow shaped our views of self-control. *Psych Central*. Retrieved on November 24, 2013, from http://psychcentral.com/blog/archives/2012/05/22/history-of-psychology-how-a-marshmallow-shaped-our-views-of-self-control/

[14] Kim, Christine. (September 22, 2008). Academic success begins at home: How children can succeed in school. *The Heritage Foundation*. Backgrounder #2185 on Education. *Retrived* September 25, 2013, from www.heritage.org/research/reports/2008/09/academic-success-begins-at-home-how-children-can-succeed-in-school

[15] Slaughter, Anne-Marie. (July/August 2012). Why women still can't have it all. The Atlantic. Retrieved September 25, 2013, from http://www.theatlantic.com/magazine/archive/2012/07/why-women-still-cant-have-it-all/309020/

[16] Haiman, Peter Ernest, Ph.D. (n.d.). Protecting a child's emotional development when parents separate or divorce. *PeterHaiman.com*. Retrieved November 30, 2013, from

ENDNOTES

www.peterhaiman.com/articles/protecting-a-childs-emotional-development-when-parents-divorce.shtml

[17] Refer to Legal Disclaimer.

[18] Bray, Llona, J.D. (n.d.). Penalties for committing immigration marriage fraud. *Nolo.com*. Retrieved November 30, 2013, from http://www.nolo.com/legal-encyclopedia/free-books/fiance-marriage-visa-book/chapter1-9.html

[19] Common law marriage. [Def. 1]. (1990). *Black's Law Dictionary*. p. 227. 6th ed.

[20] Koco.com. (February 6, 2013). Oklahoma covenant marriage bill approved in Senate Committee. *Koco.com*. Retrieved December 30, 2013, from www.koco.com/news/politics/Oklahoma-covenant-marriage-bill-approved-in-Senate-Committee/-/9843896/18431282/-/uygnbxz/-/index.html

[21] Social Security Administration. (n.d.). *What is the best age to start your benefits?*. Retrieved December 30, 2013, from, http://www.socialsecurity.gov/retire2/otherthings.htm

[22] Reagan, Michael. (n.d.). Defending families against forced no-fault divorce. *marysadvocates.org*. Retrieved January 1, 2014, from www.marysadvocates.org/michaelreagan.html

[23] Source unknown.

[24] The Church of England. (1662). The form of solemnization of matrimony. Book of Common Prayer. Retrieved December 30, 2013, from, www.pemberley.com/janeinfo/compraym.html

25 Cleave [Def. 1]. (2001-2013). Testament Hebrew Entry for Strong's #1692 – Cleave. Studylight.org. Retrieved December 30, 2013, from www.studylight.org/lex/heb/hwview.cgi?n=1692

[26] Maltby, Anna. (July, 2012). The benefits of being married. MensHealth.com. Retrieved December 30, 2013, from www.menshealth.com/mhlists/benefits_of_marriage_and_commitment/index.php

[27] Humorous note: This verse is one of my favorites. Imagine telling your boss that you have to take a year off to bring happiness to your wife.

THE CHRISTIAN PRENUPTIAL AGREEMENT

That's one heck of a honeymoon! And then you have to figure that in those days, the wife probably got pregnant right away, which meant nine months of morning sickness, followed by backaches and heartburn, followed by delivery and sleepless nights. Would bringing happiness to his wife even be possible?

[28] Eggerich, Emerson, Ph.D. (January 1, 2008). Love and respect. *Love and Respect Video Course.*

[29] Scofield, C.I. (November 1, 2011). The book of Ephesians. *Biblical Covenants.* Retrieved December 30, 2013, from www.ancientpath.net/Bible/NT/49_NewEphesians/Appendicies/49_eph_BiblicalCovenants_Scofield.htm

[30] This can be found at www.prepare-enrich.com.

[31] The Start Smart® Inventory is a premarital inventory driven by current research that provides a complete profile of a couple's strengths and growth areas in thirteen critical categories. It is part of a comprehensive premarital program designed to help couples develop skills for building a strong, lifelong marriage. It is available at http://www.livethelife.org/programs/premarital-programs/start-smart/. The cost of the program was $25 per couple as of the date December 2013.

[32] Stanley, S.M., Amato, P.R., Johnson, C.A., & Markman, H.J. (2006). Premarital education, marital quality, and marital stability: Findings from a large, random household survey. *Journal of Family Psychology*, 20, 1, 117-126.

[33] Hetherington, E. Mavis. (2002). *For better for worse: Divorce reconsidered.* Cited in Marriage, Family, and Stepfamily Statistics. Retrieved January 2, 2014, from www.smartstepfamilies.com/view/statistics

[34] http://www.abortionbreastcancer.com/

[35] Harms, Roger W., M.D. (n.d.). Abortion: Does it affect subsequent pregnancies? *Mayo Clinic Staff.* Retrieved November 26, 2011, from www.mayoclinic.com/health/abortion/AN00633

[36] Fraiman, Stephanie. (March 7, 2013). TheKnot.com and WeddingChannel.com reveal results of largest wedding study of its kind,

surveying more than 17,500 brides. *Yahoo Finance.* Retrieved November 29, 2013, from http://finance.yahoo.com/news/theknot-com-weddingchannel-com-reveal-141000109.html;_ylt=AwrNUbBozzhRqEUALuDQtDMD

[37] Thomas, Gary. (2000). *Sacred marriage: What if God designed marriage to make us holy more than to make us happy?* Grand Rapids, MI: Zondervan

[38] Ramsey, Dave. (n.d.). What does the Bible say about money? *Dave Ramsey's Financial Peace University.* Retrieved December 3, 2013, from https://crc.daveramsey.com/index.cfm?event=dspPastorExt&intContentlD=10320

[39] Barnhouse, Donald G. (1961). *God's freedom.* (p. 191). Grand Rapids, MI: Ms. B. Erdmans Publishing Company, Cited in Showers.

[40] Atomic Scale Design Network. Chemistry of love. *ASDN.net.* Retrieved November 27, 2013, from www.asdn.net/asdn/chemistry/chemistry_of_love.shtml

[41] Fisher, Helen E. (April 1, 1992). The biology of attraction. *Psychology Today.* Sussex Publishers, LLC. Retrieved November 27, 2013, from www.psychologytoday.com/articles/199303/the-biology-attraction.

[42] Fisher

[43] Ananthaswamy, Anil. (May 5, 2004). Hormones converge for couples in love. *New Scientist Online Magazine,* Retrieved November 27, 2013, from www.newscientist.com/article/dn4957-hormones-converge-for-couples-in-love.html#.UpX8ik2A270

[44] ASDN

[45] Obringer, Lee Ann. (February 12, 2005). How love works. *HowStuffWorks.com.* Retrieved December 30, 2013, from http://people.howstuffworks.com/love.htm

[46] Brown, Kathryn. (July 31, 1999). Love sick. *New Scientist.* Edition 2197. Retrieved December 30, 2013, from http://community.fortunecity.ws/underworld/continue/56/lovesick.html

[47] Buzzle. (March 27, 2004). The chemistry of love. *Buzzle.com*. Retrieved November 27, 2013, from www.buzzle.com/editorials/3-27-2004-52238.asp.

[48] Thrasybule, Linda. (February 13, 2012). Falling in love affects brain much like addiction, scientists say. *Huffington Post*. Retrieved November 27, 2013, from www.huffingtonpost.com/2012/02/13/falling-in-love-triggers-brain-changes_n_1273196.html

[49] Heussner, Ki Mae. (July 8, 2010). Addicted to love? It's not you, it's your brain. *ABC News*. Retrieved November 27, 2013, from http://abcnews.go.com/Technology/addicted-love-brain/story?id=11110866

[50] Buzzle.

[51] Buzzle.

[52] Gungor, Mark. (March 16, 2009). The damage of sexual promiscuity. *Laugh Your Way to a Better Marriage*. Retrieved December 30, 2013, from www.laughyourway.com/blog/the-damage-of-sexual-promiscuity/

[53] Teachman, Jay. (May 2003). Premarital sex, premarital cohabitation, and the risk of subsequent marital dissolution among women. *The Journal of Marriage and Family*, Vol 65, Issue 2, Pages 432-443.

[54] The Heritage Foundation. (June 23, 2003). *The harmful effects of early sexual activity and multiple sexual partners among women: A book of charts.* The Heritage Foundation. Retrieved December 30, 2013, from http://s3.amazonaws.com/thf_media/2003/pdf/Bookofcharts.pdf

[55] The Social Pathologist. (September 16, 2010). Sexual partner divorce risk. *The Social Pathologist*. Retrieved December 30, 2013, from http://socialpathology.blogspot.com/2010/09/sexual-partner-divorce-risk.html

[56] Hilton, Donald, Jr., M.D. (Summer 2010). Slave master: How pornography drugs & changes your brain. *Salvo*. Ed 13. Retrieved December 30, 2013, from

ENDNOTES

www.salvomag.com/new/articles/salvo13/13hilton.php#sthash.VSZYhG
OO.dpuf

So God created mankind in his own image,

in the image of God he created them;

male and female he created them.

God blessed them and said to them,

"Be fruitful and increase in number; fill the earth

and subdue it."

(Genesis 1:27-28a)